D0131070

TURNING POINTS IN HISTORY

GENERALS

WHO CHANGED THE WORLD

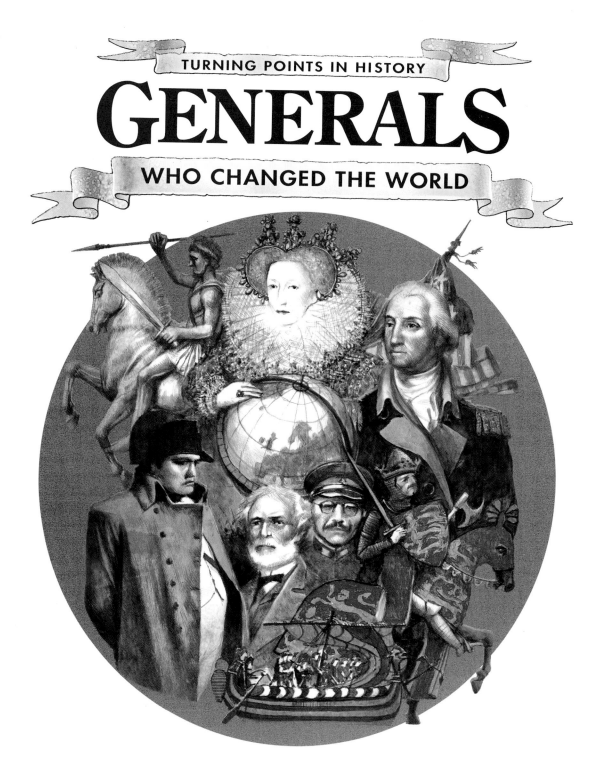

Philip Wilkinson & Michael Pollard
Illustrations by Robert Ingpen

CHELSEA HOUSE PUBLISHERS
New York • Philadelphia

First published in the United States by
Chelsea House Publishers, 1994

First Printing
1 3 5 7 9 8 6 4 2

Simplified text and captions by **Michael Pollard**
based on the *Encyclopedia of World Events*
by Robert Ingpen & Philip Wilkinson

Editor	Diana Briscoe
Project Editor	Paul Bennett
Designer	Design 23
Design Assistant	Victoria Furbisher
DTP Manager	Keith Bambury
Editorial Director	Pippa Rubinstein

ISBN 0–7910–2761–9

Printed in Italy.

Contents

Introduction

We live in a world where most people want to be at peace. After the great upheavals of the two World Wars and the conflicts in the Middle East and Africa, cries for peace seem louder than they have been for years. But we still need to understand what drove the great generals and the wars in which they fought. Battles have often changed the fate of kingdoms and empires, and they offer special insights into the way people used to live and what they considered important.

Some of the most famous military leaders have been the conquerors – men who were both king and general – driven by ambition to extend their power and influence as far as possible. Alexander the Great became king of Macedonia in Greece in 336 B.C. When he died in 323 B.C., he had conquered an area that ran from the Balkans to the Sudan, and from the shores of the Mediterranean to the plains of India.

Equally important in changing the

The Roman Empire in the West fell to barbarian invaders like the Vandals.

Mongol armies conquered most of Asia for Genghis Khan.

Drake destroyed the Armada with fire ships to prevent it from invading England.

A.D. 251   1206   1588

world are the liberators and defenders, who stood up to their oppressors. Sir Francis Drake, who led the attack on the Spanish Armada, or John Sobietski, who saved Vienna from the Ottoman advance, fall into this category. More recently, the Allies who fought against Hitler and his Third Reich, wanted a world safe from the oppressions of the Nazis, under whom whole peoples were facing genocide.

War is never really glorious: death, destruction, and misery follow it. So great generals must always be inspiring leaders – if people are to die for you, they must feel it is worthwhile. There are horrors here: the massacres of Muslims by Christians during the First Crusade, the appalling loss of life in World War I. But there are positive things too, like the end of slavery and the beginning of citizenship for black people in the U.S. after the Civil War.

Philip Wilkinson

Washington led the American colonists against their British rulers in the first modern war of independence.

Napoleon Bonaparte conquered most of Europe between 1795 and 1815.

The tide turned in World War II on the Normandy beaches, when the Allies invaded France.

1781

1812   *1944*

Alexander's Campaigns

*Astride his huge black charger, Bucephalus, the young Alexander
of Macedonia led his armies across Asia to conquer an empire
that stretched from Greece and Egypt to the plains of India.
One of the most skilful and courageous generals that the world has ever known,
his achievements are still remembered.*

| 400 | BC/AD | 400 | 800 | 1200 | 1600 | 2000 |

323 BC Hydaspes, Pakistan

In the spring of 334 B.C., a huge Greek army assembled on the western bank of the Dardanelles, the narrow sea channel that divides Europe from Asia. Under Alexander's command, there were 30,000 foot soldiers and 5,000 cavalry. They were battle-hardened troops who had fought with Alexander and his father Philip II to unite the city-states of Greece. Most important of all, they respected and almost worshiped their leader for his courage.

First target
Hundreds of warships and merchant vessels gathered to carry this mighty army across the water to the coast of present-day Turkey. It was the start of Alexander's empire-building, and Alexander himself was the first to leap from the leading ship onto foreign soil.

Alexander (356–323 B.C.) became king of Macedonia when he was 19 and soon ruled the other states of Greece. Then he set out to conquer the known world.

Alexander's first target was the land of the Greeks' great enemies and rivals, the Persians. The Persian empire, ruled by King Darius III, stretched in a wide band from Egypt, at the eastern end of the Mediterranean, to the valley of the Indus River in India.

The Persians' fatal mistake
The Persians were well prepared for the Greek invasion. Their plan was to let Alexander's soldiers land and then meet them in battle at the Granicus River, not far from the landing place. On one side of the river, in position on the steep bank, was King Darius's 40,000-strong army. But the Persians made a fatal mistake. Their cavalry were positioned along the bank, which meant that they could not

charge into the attack and drive the invaders back into the water.

Hand-to-hand combat

As always, Alexander led the Greeks into battle to the sound of trumpets and shouts to the gods. It was a bitter fight. Many Greek soldiers were cut down as they struggled out of the water, but as more made the crossing, a fierce hand-to-hand struggle developed. While the Persians strove to drive the Greeks back into the water, Alexander's troops pushed forward to force the Persians away from the riverbank and into open ground. Slowly, the better training and weapons of the Greeks began to tell, and the Persians were driven back with heavy casualties.

A trap in the mountains

Granicus was not the decisive battle against the Persians. This came in the following autumn when, after a triumphant march through Persian territory, Alexander came to the mountainous region of Issus. As Alexander's great strength lay in his cavalry, Darius had decided to wait for him in the mountains where cavalry would find it difficult to maneuver.

Again, the Persians, led by King Darius, were in formation on the farther bank of a river, behind barricades. Astride his charger, Alexander led his cavalry forward steadily, keeping them in perfect formation beyond the range of the Persian archers. Then, as the first arrows began to fly, the Greeks broke into a swift gallop. The sudden move surprised the Persians, who fled for their lives. By the time darkness fell, the battle of Issus was over. Alexander

Darius III, last ruler of the Achaemenid kingdom of Persia.

FASCINATING FACTS

Alexander founded more than 70 cities. Many of them were named Alexandria after him. Alexandria at the mouth of the River Nile became the greatest trading city of the ancient world.

———————— ❑ ————————

Alexander's horse, Bucephalus, carried Alexander throughout his Persian campaign. He died, still on duty, in India at the age of 30. Alexander gave his name to a new Indian city, Bucephala.

———————— ❑ ————————

Once he had conquered Persia, Alexander adopted the lifestyle and dress of the Persian emperor and married a number of Persian wives. One of them was Stateira, the eldest daughter of King Darius III.

———————— ❑ ————————

Unusually for men of his time, Alexander did not wear a beard. This set the fashion for Greek and Roman men for the next 500 years.

———————— ❑ ————————

Alexander used to sit up drinking all night, and sometimes did things he was sorry for when he was sober again. Once when he was drunk he set fire to the city of Persepolis!

———————— ❑ ————————

After Alexander's death, the empire became split up, for no one was strong enough to hold all the various parts of it together.

had captured Darius's headquarters together with his wife and family. Darius himself escaped into the night to fight again, but after Issus the Persian empire began to crumble.

There were more battles to come, but by 332 B.C., Alexander had moved south and east into Egypt. There, he conquered the Persians and founded cities of his own. One of these was Alexandria, which can be visited today.

Alexander the unstoppable

The next year he finally defeated Darius at the battle of Gaugamela. It seemed that the Greek general was unstoppable. Onward his men marched through eastern Persia. Some of his officers urged Alexander to stop there and be satisfied with the land he had conquered. But he ordered his army to press on eastward. In front of them lay the wild, mountainous country of the Hindu Kush.

In the spring of 338 B.C., Alexander's troops, their equipment carried by trains of camels and elephants, began the crossing of the Hindu Kush. Above their path, the mountains were capped with snow. As it melted, the streams became torrents that brought down rocks that blocked the way ahead. Many of the Greeks' horses were so tired that they died and had to be replaced by horses seized from local tribesmen. On some of these looting expeditions, Greek soldiers were set upon and killed.

Once Alexander was trapped on his own inside the walls of a city that his army was attacking. Despite the best efforts of the defenders, he fought his way to the gates and let in his army. However, he was often merciful to the people he conquered, which was unusual in those times.

The army turned north to cross the Indus at what Alexander thought would be a narrow point. But the river was too wide and deep to cross without a bridge. Alexander ordered his men to build one – a floating bridge made of the soldiers' tents filled with branches and dry leaves and sewn up to be watertight. It took the army five days to cross.

Fierce resistance
Once across the Indus, the Greeks met fierce resistance from the Indian peoples. But they pressed on north as far as Tashkent, and then marched eastward. No one knew what lay ahead. Some believed that they would come to the mythical river that, the Greeks believed, surrounded the world. But Alexander's troops were tired. Some had not seen their homes for ten years. They had endured long marches through hostile territory and the hardships of the Hindu Kush, as well as the heat of battle. And they had faced blazing heat, sandstorms, and near-starvation.

Now, as they faced yet another river-crossing of the Hydaspes, east of the Indus, the troops' discipline broke and they refused to go on. Alexander pleaded with them, urged them, and ordered them to carry on and follow him, but they refused. They had had enough. For three days the great general and his soldiers were locked in argument. Finally, Alexander gave way. The long march east was over, and it was time to return home. On the way back, as before, Alexander rode at the head of his men.

Conqueror of the known world
All Alexander's adult life had been spent in conquest, and he could not rest now. He planned further expeditions in North Africa and into mainland Europe, but these were not to be. In 323 B.C., only a year after his return from India, he was taken ill at a banquet and died a few days later. He was only 32, but he had conquered the known world. There is a story that every soldier in his army passed by his body to wish him farewell.

Alexander's soldiers came from all the different countries that he had conquered. However, most of his generals were Greeks.

Vandals, Huns, & Visigoths

Hunger was ravaging the steppes of Asia. Drought had forced the nomadic tribesmen to travel westward in search of new pastures. Eventually their travels took them across the borders of the Roman Empire. The barbarians encountered civilization and decided they wanted a share. By the time they had taken it, the Roman Empire lay in ruins.

| 400 | BC/AD | 400 | 800 | 1200 | 1600 | 2000 |

251 AD Rome, Italy

The Huns, Visigoths, and Vandals were just three of the tribes who roamed across Europe between the third and fifth centuries A.D. The Romans called all these tribes "barbarians," meaning wild people without learning or religion.

The traveling raiders

The spread of the barbarians into Europe began with the Huns of central Asia. The Huns were a tribe of people who lived on the grassy plains north of India and China. They were nomads, which meant they traveled about with their herds of sheep and goats, moving on when their animals had eaten all the grass or when they were attacked by rival tribes. By A.D. 200, they were beginning to raid the northern villages and farms of China, and in 220 they overran the

Alaric (c. A.D. 370–410) was the leader of the Visigoths who first attacked Rome in A.D. 408. In August 410, at the third attempt, he managed to occupy the city.

whole country. The Huns did not stop there. Over the next two centuries, they spread across southern Asia into Europe until, by about 400, they had arrived at the river Danube in present-day Hungary. But the valley of the Danube was already occupied by another barbarian tribe, the Visigoths. The movement of tribes within Europe began to intensify. The Huns took over the land of the Visigoths. The Visigoths attacked another group of people to the west, the Vandals. Then the Visigoths and Vandals both turned on the prosperous state of Rome.

Darkness over Europe

All the barbarian tribes were ruthless. They cared nothing for the rule of law. The barbarians' chaos and lawlessness replaced the Romans' sense of order.

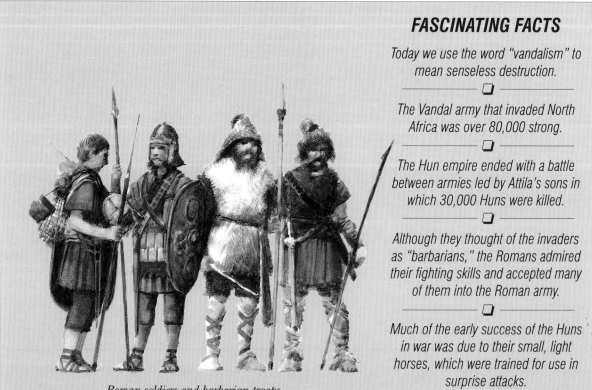
Roman soldiers and barbarian troops.

This was the start of a period in Europe known as the Dark Ages.

As they moved westward, the barbarians began to be less nomadic and to take on the lifestyles of the civilizations they had conquered. Although the spirit of war and conquest remained in their blood, they began to farm the land in a more settled way. They developed craft skills, particularly in metalwork. They also began to organize themselves into communities ruled by leaders or chieftains. In time, these leaders became recognized as kings.

On the rampage

Alaric I was chosen as king of the Visigoths in 395 when he was about 25 years old. By this time, the Roman Empire had divided in two, with the capital of the eastern half in Constantinople. Alaric I had served in the army of the eastern empire, where he had learned the skills of war. When he became king, he set about building a Visigoth empire. First he invaded Greece, but was driven out. Then, in 401, he invaded Italy. His aim was not to destroy the Roman Empire, but to share in its prosperity.

Alaric's campaign in Italy lasted for nine years. Twice, he surrounded Rome and tried to starve its people into surrender, without success. In his third attack, his troops stormed the city and went on a six-day rampage.

Alaric's plans were not yet complete. He marched his troops southward to Sicily, intending to use the island as a base for attacking North Africa, the source of Rome's grain supplies. But the Visigoth invasion fleet was wrecked in a storm. Shortly afterward, Alaric died, but the Visigoths' struggle for power in southern Europe continued.

The best-known leader of the Huns was Attila. He and his brother Bleda became kings of the Huns in 434, but eleven years later Bleda died, and Attila ruled on his own.

The savage Huns

From his capital in Hungary, Attila mounted a series of campaigns aimed at subduing the Visigoths and other tribes and forcing them to join him. His troops became notorious for their savage fighting and their cruelty, and Attila himself was feared throughout Europe. By 447, he had conquered southeastern Europe from the Black Sea to the Mediterranean, and then turned his attention westward.

The people of western Europe felt safe behind the barrier of the river Rhine, but in the spring of 451, Attila crossed the river with a huge army. They marched west, plundering and destroying the cities and countryside in their path and spreading terror among the people. Almost without opposition, Attila's army reached the French city of Orleans and surrounded it.

It looked as if the whole of France was about to come under the rule of the Huns, but the people of Orleans were saved by a combined Roman and Visigoth army. Attila had to turn away from the city to meet his attackers in an all-day battle that was one of the fiercest in history. Both sides fought without mercy, but although the

Attila's troops were fearless fighters who stopped at nothing in their march across Europe.

Visigoth king was killed, Attila was finally forced to retreat. If the Huns had continued their advance across France, the history of western Europe would have been very different.

Rome is sacked

The Vandals had been driven out of central Europe by the Huns and moved south in search of new territory. They finally settled in the Roman territory of North Africa. There they overran the Roman cities, including the capital, Carthage.

The Vandal king, Gaiseric, set out to make Carthage the center of an empire covering the whole of the Mediterranean. He built a powerful fleet of ships whose raids as far east as Greece terrorized southern Europe. In 455, Gaiseric's fleet set sail on their biggest adventure yet, an attack on Rome. Sailing up the river Tiber, they captured the city and ran wild for two weeks, stealing anything of value that they could find before sailing away. When Gaiseric died in 477, he left behind an empire that stretched all along the North African coast and into the Mediterranean.

Meanwhile, the power of Rome had finally ended. In 476, the Visigoths attacked again, and Romulus Augustulus, the Roman emperor, was removed from the throne. The eastern empire continued for another thousand years, but Rome's days of glory were over.

The movement of tribes from central Europe eventually led to the fall of Rome. Battles between the forces of the Roman Empire and barbarian armies were often very bloody and led to the destruction and looting of cities as the barbarians rampaged through the streets.

Viking Raiders & Conquerors

"Save us from the fury of the Northmen!" was the desperate prayer of the people across Europe for over two hundred years.
Sighting the Vikings' longships with their dragon prows struck terror into the hearts of warriors from Cornwall to Byzantium.
They knew how terrible the Vikings were in their "berserk" battle rages.

400	BC/AD	400	800	1200	1600	2000

911 AD Normandy, France

The Vikings came by sea from Denmark, Norway, and Sweden. The sight of their longships approaching the coast struck terror into the hearts of local people. The ferocious Vikings attacked monasteries, towns, and cities, plundering them for precious stones and metals and other valuables. Often, they left behind smoldering ruins and the families of prisoners taken home as slaves.

Terror ships
Even inland cities were not safe. For example, in A.D. 845 a force of 120 Viking longships sailed up the River Seine in France and attacked Rouen and Paris. It was the first of many inland raids in northern France. Viking expeditions along Europe's other great rivers, such as the Rhine, Danube, and Volga, followed.

This chessman represents a mounted Viking warrior. The Vikings were the best-equipped warriors of their time, and had the fastest and most powerful warships afloat.

With their superior ships – their longships had a large, square sail and as many as eighty oarsmen each, which made them the fastest and most powerful warships afloat – and their ruthless fighting methods, the Vikings could attack wherever they liked. Their weapons – axes, throwing-hammers, spears, javelins, bows and arrows, and swords – were without doubt the best in Europe.

The Vikings were unafraid of death, and sometimes in the midst of battle they were overcome by a fighting madness that was known as going "berserk," a word we use today to mean frenziedly violent or destructive.

The raids begin
The first Viking raid, in 793, was on the island monastery of Lindisfarne off the

coast of northern England.

Over the next century, the Vikings sailed farther and farther in search of loot, attacking as far south as Spain and Italy and as far east as Russia and the Black Sea. But it was not only loot that attracted the Vikings. They had a great thirst for exploration and adventure.

Viking empire

The first raiders were pirates and robbers who simply took what they wanted and sailed home. But later the aim of the Vikings changed. The farming land in their own countries was overcrowded, and they needed more space. The pirates brought back news of the rich soil of mainland Europe, ideal for Vikings to capture and settle in.

More highly organized bands of Vikings now began to spend the winter in camps close to the coasts of the invaded territory, moving outward in spring to occupy the land. By 840, there were Viking settlements in Ireland, and by 900 others had spread down the northwestern coast of Europe from the Netherlands to northern France, and across the North Sea into eastern Britain.

Toward the end of the ninth century, Danes began to invade southern England and might have conquered it had it not been for the king of Wessex (a kingdom in south and southwest England) and overlord of England, Alfred the Great, who defeated the Danes.

The Vikings also settled in Iceland and southwest Greenland. It was these Greenland Vikings that went in search of land to the west and landed on a part of the North American coast

where the winters were mild, probably between Nova Scotia and Cape Cod.

Christian converts

The countries that the Vikings invaded were Christian. Most of them had been part of the Roman Empire. The Viking raiders had their own religion and their own gods. They destroyed Christian churches and monasteries and stole their valuables. But when the Vikings settled in Christian countries, they often became Christians themselves.

According to legend, one Viking, Olaf Tryggvason, spent the early part of his life raiding and plundering. But then he came to the Isles of Scilly, where he was converted to Christianity by a hermit.

One of the most successful of the Viking leaders, or chieftains, who became a Christian was called Rollo. He was probably a Dane, and he led a

series of attacks on northern France in about 900. Sometimes his army was defeated, but he returned to the attack again and again.

By 911, Rollo had forced the king of France to make him Duke of Normandy and had taken over northern France for the Vikings. The "Northmen" had become the Normans, and they, too, 150 years later, would set out to invade England and conquer it.

From the eighth to eleventh centuries A.D., the coasts of eastern Europe were raided by fierce warriors who came to plunder and, later, to conquer land for themselves and settle down as farmers. The Vikings caused great misery on their raids, for they killed people and burnt their homes, drove away their cattle, and robbed churches of their treasures. The legends the Vikings told about their heroes and gods inspired them in battle, and they were famed for their fighting skill and fearlessness, which made them too strong to be resisted.

William I Conquers England

Descendant of Vikings, a bastard who had had to battle the barons for his inheritance, Duke William of Normandy believed he had been promised the throne of England, and he was ready to fight for what was his. His success linked the fortunes of England and France for the next 500 years.

| 400 | BC/AD | 400 | 800 | | 1200 | 1600 | 2000 |

1066 Hastings, England

Duke William of Normandy, or William the Conqueror, had to endure a long and frustrating wait in Normandy. It was 1066 and his soldiers and ships were ready to invade England, but the wind blew steadily from the north. Until it changed direction, the Norman fleet could not sail across the Channel.

Rivals for the throne
Earlier in 1066, King Edward of England had died. His crown went to Harold, his brother-in-law, but two other men wanted to rule England. Duke William believed that he had been promised the throne when Edward died. Harald Hardrada, the Viking king of Norway, also claimed the throne and planned to invade England himself.

The north wind that

William the Conqueror (c.1027–87) was a proud and ruthless ruler. Born out of wedlock, he succeeded as duke when only a child. He spent years subduing his barons (nobles).

kept William in port was just right for a voyage from Norway, and in September Harald Hardrada's soldiers landed in Yorkshire. The English army hurried north to meet them and defeated the Vikings at Stamford Bridge, near York. But by this time, the wind had changed, and the Normans were able to sail across the English Channel. They landed on the beach at Pevensey, near Hastings, on September 28 – three days after Harold's victory over the Vikings.

During the Battle of Hastings, King Harold was slain and the massed ranks of his troops broken up by William's spearmen and cavalry. After this, William marched on London, finding enough support among the English lords to be crowned king, establishing Norman rule in England.

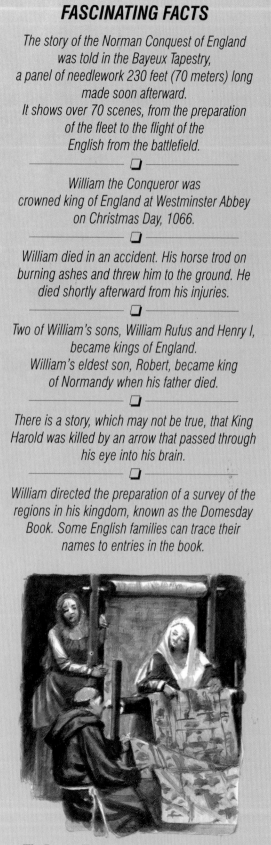
The Normans, encamped on the English shore, were able to rest and prepare themselves for battle. The English troops were tired – they had marched 250 miles (400 kilometers) from Yorkshire – and their wounded had been replaced on the way south by new recruits who had never experienced battle.

The two sides met north of Hastings on October 14. Duke William's cavalry, armed with spears and bows, faced an English army made up almost entirely of foot soldiers. Duke William was almost 30 and had fought many victorious battles against rebels in Normandy. Although Harold was about ten years older, he had less experience of warfare.

The Normans' trick

The English took up their positions on a hill and formed a wall of shields against the enemy. At about nine o'clock in the morning, the Normans' cavalry attacked, but the wall of English shields held firm. Norman cavalry tried again to break through, but each time they were driven back. Then the Normans, pretending to retreat, tempted the English to move forward.

The English troops fell for the trick and met a hail of arrows, one of which killed King Harold. Still they bravely held on for several hours. But finally night came, and the few English survivors retreated to the safety of the nearby forest – William had won.

William's victory changed the way of life for people in England. For many years, Norman rule was harsh and cruel. But William the Conqueror's invasion marked the beginning of the growth of England into one of the leading nations of Europe.

Ghana Falls to the Almoravids

*The Empire of Ghana was rich in gold and salt, slaves and ivory.
Its people worshiped the unseen spirits — an abomination to the Muslim
warriors of the Sahara who followed Allah, the One God.
They launched a jihad against the infidels and so destroyed a great
African civilization, as they converted the people of West Africa to Islam.*

400	BC/AD	400	800		1200	1600	2000

1075 Kumbi Saleh, Mauritania

We must not confuse the ancient African kingdom of Ghana with modern Ghana, which is a state on the west coast of Africa. Ancient Ghana was an inland country about 500 miles (800 kilometers) to the northwest of modern Ghana.

Important trading centers

Founded by black tribespeople in about A.D. 600, ancient Ghana grew quickly in wealth and importance. Its two major cities, Audagost and the capital, Kumbi, became the most important trading centers in west Africa. As well as gold and salt, Ghana traded in ivory, slaves, ostrich feathers, and animal hides. The kings of Ghana grew rich from the taxes they charged on goods passing through their markets.

To the north of ancient Ghana lay the wastes of the Sahara and,

*Abu Bakr became leader of the Almoravids in 1056.
Soon afterward, he began his military campaign to capture Ghana for the Islamic religion.*

beyond the desert, the Mediterranean coastal region of what is now Morocco. This was the country of the Almoravids, a tribe which had been converted to Islam – the religion of Muslims, founded by Muhammad.

The Almoravids had a well-armed and highly trained army. Their infantry carried javelins and pikes and were supported by regiments of cavalry on horses and camels. When Abu Bakr became the Almoravids' leader in 1056, he decided to lead this army south to capture Ghana.

Preparing for success

The Almoravids were devout followers of Islam. At least part of their aim in attacking Ghana was to convert the kingdom's people to the religion. There is a story that Abu Bakr prepared himself for this task by shutting

himself away with a handful of trusted followers on an island in the river Senegal, to the west of Ghana. There, he fasted and prayed for success. Then he returned to collect his army, and in about 1062 he set out for conquest.

Stiff resistance

The Almoravids were fierce warriors and merciless conquerors. They took command of defeated tribes' land, stole their possessions, made each person pay taxes to support the army, and forced them to become Muslims. But they met stiff resistance from the people of Ghana, and their advance was slow. Abu Bakr seized the city of

Abu Bakr planned to capture Ghana and convert the people to Islam. His Almoravid army was trained in monasteries that combined religious and military teaching.

Audagost soon after the start of his campaign, but it was not until 1076, twenty years later, that he conquered Ghana's capital, Kumbi.

The Almoravid attacks did not bring the old kingdom of Ghana to an end at once. The Almoravids began to quarrel among themselves and failed to take advantage of their military victories. But warfare had disrupted travel and trading, and merchants began to look for other, more peaceful routes across the desert and markets to buy and sell their wares.

A much weaker, poorer Ghana struggled on until about 1230, when it was invaded finally from the west. But the Almoravid invasion had left behind the Islamic faith, which spread outward from Ghana to almost the whole of west Africa.

FASCINATING FACTS

Almoravid rule in northwest Africa lasted until 1147, when another Islamic tribal group, the Almohads, took their place.

Salt – then the main way of preserving meat – was so scarce in west Africa that many merchants in Ghana would exchange it only for gold.

Travel across the Sahara Desert, even in large camel trains, was dangerous. Travelers depended on obtaining water at oases – places in the desert where water is found and trees grow (below). If these dried up, hundreds of traders and their camels could die of thirst. Their skeletons often lay beside the tracks for years.

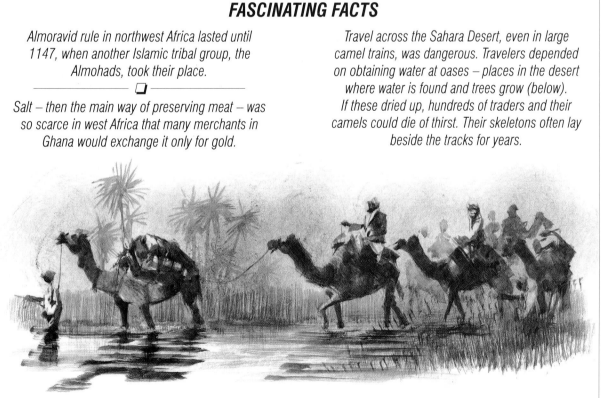

The First Crusade

"Take the cross!" cried Urban II in 1095. "Rise up and fight for the Holy Land,
join the crusade and free Jerusalem from the infidels."
Across Europe, more than 100,000 people heard his call and responded.
They set out with noble ideals, but their deeds did not match –
Christian and Muslim antagonism grew even greater from their atrocities.

400	BC/AD	400	800		1200	1600	2000

1099 Jerusalem, Israel

One thousand years ago, most of western Europe was made up of the powerful Holy Roman Empire. This empire was Christian and looked to the Pope in Rome as its leader. To the east was the Byzantine Empire. Based on Constantinople in what is now Turkey, this was the eastern half of the old Roman Empire and it followed the Greek Orthodox faith, a form of Christianity. And stretching from the eastern Mediterranean through North Africa to southern Spain, there were the states of Islam, Muslim followers of the prophet Muhammad.

Tension

To Christians, the area of the eastern Mediterranean where the events described in the New Testament of the Bible took place was the "Holy Land." At the heart of

A crusader at prayer. Although they claimed to be fighting for their religious beliefs, many crusaders were more interested in seizing land and treasures.

the Holy Land was Jerusalem, which for 400 years had been in Islamic territory. Christians from the Holy Roman Empire would have to travel through the territory of the Byzantine Empire to recapture it from the Muslims. The situation was like a bonfire waiting for a spark to set it alight.

The flame of war

The pope, Urban II (c. 1035–1099), provided the spark that set the bonfire of war alight. In a sermon preached in 1095 at Clermont in France, he urged Christians to join in a holy war to free Jerusalem from Islamic rule and return it to the Christians.

The Pope's call caused excitement throughout Europe. Christians everywhere began to prepare for the long march to Jerusalem. They called themselves "crusaders." The name came from *crux*, the Latin word for the cross on which Jesus Christ had died. The crusaders carried the sign of the cross on their uniforms and banners.

Peasants and nobles

There were two main groups of crusaders. One was made up of poor people. Its leaders, such as the monks Peter the Hermit and Walter the Penniless, were themselves poor. They were full of enthusiasm for the crusade, but they had no idea of what would be involved. They thought that their Christian beliefs would make up for their lack of experience in warfare and their lack of weapons.

The second group was made up of cavalry and infantry, commanded by French noblemen. This was a well-trained and well-equipped force. Its leader was Duke Godfrey of Bouillon (c.1060–1100) from the Ardennes, France.

As they travelled southeastward across Europe, both groups picked up more followers. On their way they had to pass through Constantinople, the Byzantine capital. By the time they arrived there, the crusaders' army was about 150,000 strong.

Slaughter and loot

Not all crusaders were driven by their religious beliefs. Some were after any land or loot they could gain on the way. Others were out for adventure.

The poor crusaders' journey across Europe was marked by terrible crimes. Some of the crusaders identified the Jewish people as "enemies of Christianity," and there were mass killings of Jews in many German cities. There were more killings in Hungary

Alexius I Comnenius (1048–1118), Emperor of Byzantium.

FASCINATING FACTS

Peter the Hermit (c. 1050–c. 1115) was a poor priest whose preaching had a magical effect on those who heard him. He rode from place to place on a donkey. Peter survived the first crusade and died of old age in a monastery he had founded.

———————— ❏ ————————

Between 1096 and 1291 there were eight crusades, during which Jerusalem was taken by the Christians and recaptured by the Muslims several times. Finally the Muslims, under their great leader, Saladin (1137–93), regained control of Jerusalem in 1187.

Saracen shield with an Arabic inscription.

and Bulgaria. The cruelty of the crusaders provoked counterattacks, and many thousands of the poor crusaders deserted or were slaughtered. It was a downhearted and much smaller army that finally reached Constantinople.

The emperor's choice
Meanwhile, traveling by a different route, Duke Godfrey and his army were close to Constantinople. Now came the big question. Would the Byzantine emperor, Alexius I, join forces with the crusaders and march with them to Jerusalem? Or would he stand aside and let the Christians of the Holy Roman Empire fight it out with Islam on their own?

The crusaders did not wait to find out. Both armies – the force led by Duke Godfrey and the poor men – attacked Constantinople. But the Byzantine army soon defeated Peter the Hermit's badly organized and poorly equipped troops, and they were sent on their way through the hostile territory of the warlike Seljuk Turks. There, what was left of Peter's army was massacred, though Peter himself survived to join Duke Godfrey's army.

Meanwhile, Duke Godfrey made peace with Alexius, and a joint army of crusaders and Byzantine soldiers marched onward toward Jerusalem. On the journey they met the Seljuk Turks, but they were no match for this huge army and were soon defeated. More killings, looting, and destruction

At the Turkish stronghold of Antioch, a Turkish traitor allowed some crusaders into the city so that the gates could be opened to the crusading army. The result was a bloodbath with no Muslims spared.

marked the onward march of the crusade until, on June 7, 1099, the crusaders reached the stoutly walled city of Jerusalem.

Duke Godfrey's plan was to surround Jerusalem and then batter it into surrender. Rams would smash into the city walls, and then soldiers would pour over the damaged walls on ladders. It took a month to build the equipment Duke Godfrey needed. Few trees grew in the Holy Land, and parties of soldiers had to be sent off to find timber. Finally, on July 15, the assault came, and the Pope's prayer that Jerusalem should again be a Christian city was granted.

The capture of Jerusalem is still remembered as one of the most terrible acts of war. The crusaders killed all the Jews and almost all the Muslims they could find. The story goes that so much blood flowed in the streets that the crusaders' horses, storming through the streets, were splashed with blood to the saddles. The Christians had turned their Holy City into a city of death.

Holy wars

This was the end of the first crusade. Jerusalem was once again a city ruled by Christians. But it was the start of a series of holy wars that went on for nearly 200 years. The Christians were finally driven out of the Holy Land in 1291. But followers of Islam did not forget the bloodthirsty Christians who, in the name of the "Prince of Peace," stormed Jerusalem 900 years ago.

This map shows the boundaries of the four crusader states in about 1150.

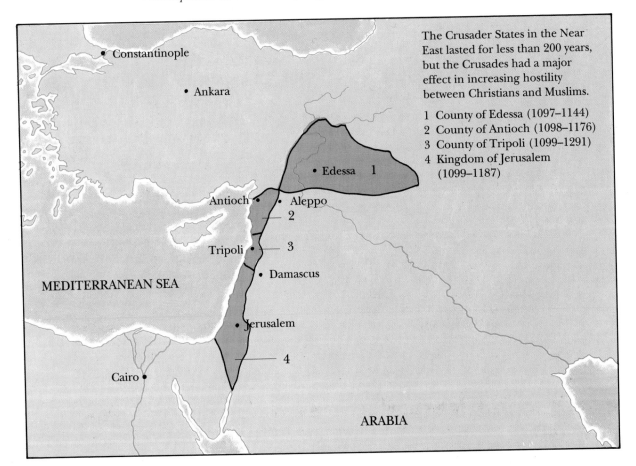

The Crusader States in the Near East lasted for less than 200 years, but the Crusades had a major effect in increasing hostility between Christians and Muslims.

1 County of Edessa (1097–1144)
2 County of Antioch (1098–1176)
3 County of Tripoli (1099–1291)
4 Kingdom of Jerusalem (1099–1187)

Genghis Khan's Mongol Hordes

Chinese officials were not concerned when reports reached them of a new leader among the Mongol tribes. They were barbarians, always fighting among themselves – things would settle down soon enough.
But this leader was different. Genghis Khan sent his horsemen out over the steppe and conquered an empire stretching from Baghdad to Beijing.

| 400 | BC/AD | 400 | 800 | 1200 | 1600 | 2000 |

1206 Qaraqorum, Mongolia

The tribe that proclaimed a man named Temuchin "Genghis Khan," or universal leader, was only one of many that made up the Mongolian people. The Mongols were nomads who roamed with their animals across the wide steppes, or plains, of northern Mongolia. They were skilled horsemen and warriors, and the tribes often fought with each other. Each tribe had its chieftain, or khan.

Rival tribes

The young Temuchin was encouraged by his mother in his ambition to become leader of all the Mongol tribes. His skill on horseback, in battle, and as a leader of his soldiers enabled him to defeat all but two rival tribes by the time he was 25. The two exceptions were the Keraits, whose leader was Wang Khan, and the Naimans, led by Polo

The battle standard of Genghis Khan (c. 1162–1227), a pole with nine yak's tails attached, which was carried ahead of his conquering army.

Khan. Of these, the Keraits were the more powerful.

Temuchin attacks

Wang Khan had been Temuchin's ally in previous tribal battles, but there was no room for both of them as leader of the Mongols. A battle was inevitable. The outcome was decided when Temuchin sent spies into the Kerait camp who pretended to negotiate about the return of prisoners. The spies reported back that Wang Khan was not ready for battle, and Temuchin ordered an immediate attack. After three days of merciless slaughter, the Keraits conceded defeat. Keyed up by this victory, Temuchin went straight on to defeat the Naimans.

It was time for Temuchin to take over leadership of all the Mongol tribes. In 1206

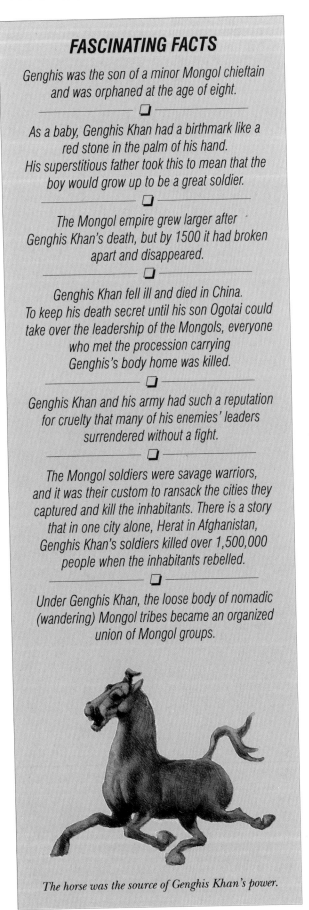

The horse was the source of Genghis Khan's power.

he called a great meeting of Mongol leaders, who proclaimed him Genghis Khan. From that time on Temuchin was always known by this name. The meeting marked a turning point in history. If the people of Asia had known what it meant, they would have trembled.

Ruthless commander

Genghis Khan now had under his command the finest fighters of all the Mongol tribes. He used them to carve out a Mongol empire across southern Asia. He was a ruthless commander, and his troops killed any enemy soldiers they captured.

There were no foot soldiers in Genghis Khan's army. Every man was a cavalryman, who rode with a spare horse for carrying baggage and lived off the countryside. The army moved in great columns many miles apart, destroying everything in their path, closing to assist each other when necessary. Cities that resisted them were destroyed and the people murdered, while cities that surrendered without a fight might be spared destruction.

Across the Great Wall

To the southeast of Mongolia lay the rich and powerful Chinese empire, and it was this that Genghis Khan

When Genghis Khan and his hordes began to arrive outside the cities of Russia in the 1220s, his empire stretched across much of Asia. Although the Russian cities were well defended, they could not withstand the force of the Mongol armies. After defeating two Russian armies in 1223, the Mongol force laid waste to the areas along the Don and Dnieper rivers and the Sea of Azov.

attacked first. He quickly conquered the Chinese province of Hsi-Hsia before crossing the Great Wall into China itself.

By taking Hsi-Hsia, Genghis Khan had an easier route eastward to China. Here, he met greater resistance – the Chinese walled cities meant that he had to adopt the use of siege machines. Although he captured Peking, the Chinese capital, in 1215, it was not until after Genghis Khan's death in 1227 that the whole of China became part of the Mongol empire.

The empire grows

Genghis Khan also led his army westward to crush the powerful Khwarezm empire, now Uzbekistan, and within a year its capital Samarkand was captured. The army then moved westward along the northern shore of the Caspian Sea into Russia and on to Persia, now Iran.

Genghis Khan suffered a fatal hunting accident while his troops were besieging a city in China. When he died on August 18, 1227, he controlled an empire that stretched across southern Asia from the Caspian Sea to Peking. But he had won it at the cost of what is said to be 18 million lives.

Genghis Khan was all-powerful in Asia, but he was not very interested in the comforts of power. He handed over day-to-day rule of his conquered lands to trusted allies. Genghis Khan remained until his death a tribal chieftain and a warrior at heart, happier in the saddle at the head of his soldiers than in a palace. However, his cruelty means that he is still named today when people want to describe a merciless, unforgiving enemy.

These tents, called yurts, *were what the Mongols lived in.*

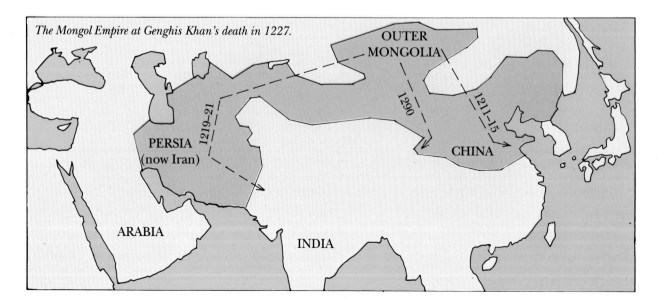

Byzantium Falls to Mehmet II

Constantinople has fallen to the Turks – the message sent a shiver through Europe as kings and churchmen realized that the last bastion of Byzantium, heir to the Roman Empire, had fallen to a Muslim conqueror. A new empire had arisen at the gates of Europe, one that was not friendly to Christians, and had altered the balance of power in the Mediterranean...

400	BC/AD	400	800	1200		1600	2000

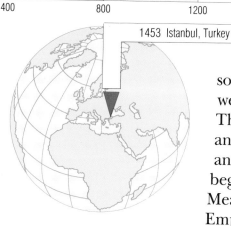

1453 Istanbul, Turkey

Constantinople, sited beside a narrow channel linking the Black Sea with the Mediterranean, was a vital link between Asia and Europe. For thousands of years, it was a crossroads for trading routes between East and West.

Rival empires

In A.D. 330, Constantinople became the capital of the Byzantine Empire, which had taken over the eastern part of the Roman Empire. The Byzantines' thousand-year history included periods of great achievement in art and architecture, but also times of great hardship, chaos, and cruelty.

By the 14th century, a new power had arisen in the region. The Ottoman Turks, originally from a mountainous area

Sultan Mehmet II (1432–81), known as "Mehmet the Conqueror," became ruler of the Ottoman Empire in 1451 and reigned for 30 years.

south of Constantinople, were followers of Islam. They were well-organized and courageous soldiers, and from about 1320 they began to build an empire. Meanwhile, the Byzantine Empire was being divided and weakened by civil wars. By about 1450, a small area near Constantinople was all that was left of Byzantium.

Destroy Constantinople!

In 1451, Mehmet II became the head of the Ottoman Empire. He was young and ambitious. His aim was to make his empire the most powerful force in the world. Weak though the Byzantines were, Constantinople stood in the way of Mehmet's plans. So he decided that Constantinople must be his.

He already controlled the surrounding land and sea and could

merely have starved the city out, but he chose to mount an all-out attack. On April 7, 1453, a huge Ottoman army assembled to the west of the city. They were fearless soldiers, but they faced an enormous challenge.

Fortress on seven hills

Constantinople was a natural fortress built on seven hills overlooking the Bosporus, the narrow neck of water joining the Black Sea with the Sea of Marmara. To the north was the Golden Horn, a superb natural harbor. Where the city faced the land, huge double walls surmounted with many towers guarded the city against attack.

Mehmet's army began its assault on Constantinople by pounding the walls with cannon. Even after seven weeks of this, the walls still held firm. So

A medieval view of Constantinople. The city had strong walls, but the Ottomans got through an open gate. In front are a court official, a falconer, and a foot soldier of Mehmet's time.

Mehmet decided to launch a second assault from the sea.

Ottoman ships were already moored in the Bosporus, and Mehmet tried to bring them round into the narrow channel of the Golden Horn. The Byzantines foiled this plan by stretching an enormous chain across the channel. But Mehmet responded by transporting his ships overland.

The gate to disaster

The end of Constantinople came on May 29 with an Ottoman attack at three separate points around the city. Even then, the city might have been saved if one small gate had not been left unguarded. Mehmet's troops swarmed through, and in a few hours the battle was over.

News of the fall of Constantinople to Islam horrified Christian Europe. It seemed as if the world had turned upside-down. Even today, the fall of Constantinople is seen as the end of a chapter in world history – the Middle Ages – and the start of another.

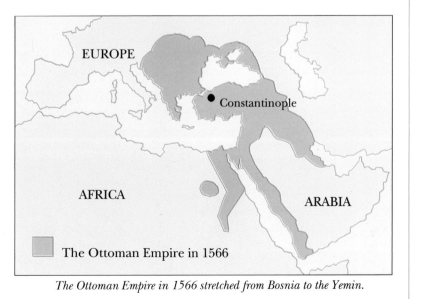

FASCINATING FACTS

The Ottoman Empire made Constantinople its capital and added many beautiful buildings. Although it was greatly weakened in its last years, the Ottoman Empire remained a world power until 1918.

❑

In 1930, Constantinople's name was changed to Istanbul. It is still Turkey's largest city and her main seaport. But since 1923 Turkey's capital city has been Ankara.

EUROPE

● Constantinople

AFRICA

ARABIA

◼ The Ottoman Empire in 1566

The Ottoman Empire in 1566 stretched from Bosnia to the Yemin.

Babur Conquers India

In 1521, a small army marched down the Khyber Pass and stormed out onto the plains of northern India. Led by Babur, a brilliant general, and armed with the new-fangled artillery, the soldiers defeated army after army until all of north India was united in a new Muslim empire. The results of this conquest can still be seen today in India and Pakistan.

| 400 | BC/AD | 400 | 800 | 1200 | ▲ 1600 | 2000 |

1526 Delhi, India

If people can be born with leadership "in their blood," Babur should have had it in his – he was descended from two great Mongol warlords. His mother was a member of Genghis Khan's family, and his father was from the family of Tamerlane the Great, the last of the Mongol empire-builders.

The roads from Samarkand
Babur was born in Persia. When the Mongols split up their empire, some of them remained in Persia and founded a new state. They were called "Mughals" by the local Persians, and Babur was born into the Mughal royal family.

The Mughals' state spread eastward beyond Persia, and Tamerlane (1336–1404) had set up its capital in Samarkand, now in the Republic of Uzbekistan. Samarkand was a key base for

Babur the Conqueror (1483–1530) was the nephew of the Sultan of Samarkand. He was only 14 when he scored his first victory in battle.

military adventures in central Asia. To the east and west ran the ancient trade route between China and the Middle East. Southward, other trade routes crossed the mountainous Hindu Kush into Afghanistan.

The Mongols of central Asia were nomadic (traveling) people who were not attracted by a settled way of life on farms or in cities. But the Mughals, when they lived among the Persians, had learned that settling down had its advantages and pleasures. This had a great influence on Babur.

Teenage general
Babur grew up with a love of Persian art, language, and culture. He also learned the skills of warfare, and first led an army into battle against rebel tribesmen when he was only 14 years old.

Babur's father had

spent his life trying to capture Samarkand from a rival prince, and Babur followed in his footsteps. Between 1494 and 1504, Babur sought to capture the city and twice occupied it, in 1497 and 1501.

However, Babur had a powerful opponent who was also a descendant of Genghis Khan, named Muhammad Shaybani Khan, and in 1501 Babur was decisively defeated and lost the city.

Kabul is captured

But Babur was a talented and ambitious young man, and he was determined to build an empire of his own. And so in 1504, when he was 21, he led his troops southeast into Afghanistan and occupied the capital, Kabul. From there he planned his next moves against Samarkand, but his last attempt, in 1511, also failed.

At that time, India was made up of a number of states, some Muslim and some Hindu. These states quarreled constantly, and in the last months of 1525 a group of princes from the Lodi Empire in northwest India asked Babur to help them defeat their rivals.

Lightning campaign

In a lightning campaign, Babur stormed through the Punjab and aimed for Delhi, the center of the most powerful state in northern India.

In 1526, he confronted the Sultan of Delhi, Ibrahim Lodi, about 60 miles (100 kilometers) north of the city of Panipat. Babur's army, only 9,000 strong, was tiny compared with the 100,000 troops and 100 elephants that the Indians could call on. But Babur had two great advantages. First, his army was equipped with artillery – new weapons unknown to the Indians.

Secondly, although the sultan's army outnumbered Babur's many times, it was poorly commanded and badly equipped. The Indian troops, whose armor consisted only of layers of cotton, were no match for Babur's heavily armored cavalry.

Babur marches into Delhi
After a hard-fought battle that lasted all day, Babur's victory was complete, and the sultan was dead. Babur marched his men on into Delhi. His first action in the city was to lay out a garden by the river Yamuna, now known as the Ram Bagh.

This was only the beginning. Using Delhi as his base, Babur went on quickly to conquer the Hindu Rajput states of northern India. In one battle, his army was surrounded by a force of about 100,000 horses and 500 elephants, but his men stood their ground using a barrier of wagons with

gaps for the artillery and for the cavalry to charge out suddenly. The artillery stampeded the elephants, and the cavalry bewildered the enemy, who after ten hours broke ranks, never to rally under a single leader again.

Babur secures his empire

Babur now had to deal with the defiant Afghans to the east, who had captured the city of Lucknow. After crossing the Ganges river he drove the Afghans out

Babur was a brilliant general who founded the Mughal Empire in India. His troops were not used to the hot Indian weather and were often heavily outnumbered by the armies they faced. But Babur's use of artillery, which stampeded the elephants his opponents used in battle, and superior cavalry tactics gave him the advantage on the battlefield. Babur was not only a great soldier, but he was also a poet and a lover of nature. He built magnificent palaces, mosques, and gardens wherever he went, and held festive parties in beautiful places.

of Lucknow. Now only Sultan Ibrahim's brother, Mahmud Lodi, stood between Babur securing an empire.

In 1529, the two opponents engaged each other next to the Ganges River. Using his artillery to good effect, Babur won the battle decisively. His empire now stretched from Kabul in Afghanistan right across to Allahabad in eastern India.

Religious tolerance

Although Babur's ancestors had been Mongols and he was every bit as courageous in battle as they had been, his behavior toward the people he had conquered was quite different. A true Mongol would have persecuted and slaughtered anyone with a different religious faith, but Babur believed in tolerance toward the Hindus who made up four-fifths of his empire's population.

Splendid buildings

Babur was also unlike his Mongol ancestors in another way. The Mongols plundered and destroyed the cities they conquered. The Mughals improved them. They created magnificent new palaces and mosques and planted beautiful gardens round them. They made space for libraries and music rooms, and they planted fruit orchards. Although they were successful warriors, they also enjoyed the pleasures of peace and leisure.

The Mughal empire founded by Babur lasted for over 300 years. When it finally declined, it left behind many splendid buildings that can still be seen today, as well as a rich culture of literature, art, and music.

Babur receives a report from one of his generals. He encouraged artists and poets to attend his court.

The Netherlanders' Revolt

In 1572, Spain controlled a large part of Europe and was immensely rich, receiving huge sums of money from her New World colonies. The Netherlands was a very small part of her empire, but the Dutch burghers were not afraid of resisting Spanish tyranny. They rose up and drove out the Spanish troops, opening the way for the people to develop into a nation.

| 400 | BC/AD | 400 | 800 | 1200 | 1600 | 2000 |

1574 Leyden, Netherlands

The Netherlands we know today has not always been a self-governing country – 600 years ago it was ruled over by Austria, for example. Then from 1504, the Netherlands came under the control of Catholic Spain, who appointed a series of governors to rule the country. The result was a long-running battle between the fiercely independent Dutch and their Spanish rulers. The Dutch resented having to pay taxes to Spain, and as Protestants (a religious group who had turned away from the Roman Catholic Church), they were not allowed by their Catholic rulers to worship as they wished.

The hard man

After an unsuccessful revolt in 1566, the Spanish king, Philip II (1527–98), sent Ferdinand, Duke of Alba, to bring order to the Netherlands. The duke was a hard man, and protesters were

William the Silent (1533–84), Count of Nassau & Prince of Orange, was chosen to lead the Dutch. He was murdered by an assassin on Spanish orders.

sentenced to death or imprisoned and tortured. Thousands more fled to Germany and England to escape punishment.

By 1572, the Dutch had had enough. The last two years had been terrible. Apart from the harsh rule of the Spanish, the harvest had failed, bringing the threat of starvation, great storms and high tides had flooded large areas of coastal farmland, and an epidemic of plague – a killer disease – broke out. The final blow came when the Duke of Alba announced a new tax of one-tenth on all sales, the "Tenth Penny," as the Dutch called it. It was time to fight.

Sea Beggars

The Dutch, who were expert seamen, had found a brilliant way of interrupting Spanish trade and gathering together a force for their rebellion. They became pirates, calling

The "United Provinces," as the Netherlands became known in 1584, included Holland, Zeeland, Brabant, Friesland, and Utrecht.

❑

To remind the Dutch of what they were fighting for, the Sea Beggars flew a flag showing ten coins, which stood for the hated "Tenth Penny" tax.

❑

Even children took part in the protests against the "Tenth Penny." In 1571, 400 children played a "Tenth Penny" counting game outside the palace of the Duke of Alba.

❑

Leyden University, which was to become one of the leading universities in Europe, was founded by William of Orange in 1575 to celebrate the departure of the Spanish.

❑

Dutch families that had escaped to Germany and England raised thousands of pounds to support the Sea Beggars and other rebel forces.

❑

The same recipe for hutspot, *or hotch-potch, is used for the dish that is eaten every year at Leyden to mark the anniversary of the Spanish departure.*

❑

The siege of Leyden was an important turning point in the Dutch revolt, but it was not until 1584 that the Netherlands, under William of Orange, became an independent state.

Spanish soldiers carrying muskets.

themselves the "Sea Beggars."

On April 1, 1572, troops carried by the Sea Beggars' fleet landed on the coast at Den Briel. The rebels now had a base from which to carry on their fight. This was the signal for towns all over the Netherlands to rise up against the Spanish.

In July 1572, the rebels proclaimed William of Orange their leader. For two years the Spanish struggled to put down the rebels, scoring some successes and some failures.

The great siege

The most famous Spanish defeat – achieved without a shot being fired – was at Leyden in 1574. In May, the Spanish began a six-month siege of the city. The people of Leyden were in a desperate state, short of food and suffering from plague. One-third of the population died.

Leyden was on low-lying land only a few miles from the sea, protected from flooding by a series of dikes. In August the rebel leaders made a desperate decision. They would break down the dikes so that seawater would flood in. A fleet of Sea Beggars stood by to sail in with troops and relief supplies for the town.

At first, it looked as if the plan would fail. Tides were low, and the wind failed to drive the sea inland. But as the storms of autumn whipped up the North Sea, the floods came. Finally, on the night of October 23, the surviving people of Leyden were able at last to celebrate. In panic and disorder, the Spanish had retreated.

A Dutch boy was the first to discover that the Spanish had retreated. He brought a pot filled with savory stew or hutspot *to prove it.*

Drake & the Spanish Armada

Beacons flared in the darkness, carrying the news to London that the invasion fleet of Philip II of Spain was in sight. The English fleet set sail from Plymouth, going up against overwhelming odds. But the fire that had warned of the Armada also destroyed it. Drake's fireships broke up the Armada's formations, and British weather destroyed the lumbering galleys.

| 400 | BC/AD | 400 | 800 | 1200 | 1600 | 2000 |

1588 English Channel

It was on May 30, 1588, that the Armada – a huge Spanish fleet of 151 ships with 20,000 men on board – set sail from Lisbon in Portugal, bound for England. King Philip II of Spain's aim was to capture Protestant England and return it to the Roman Catholic faith. The plan was not to wage a war at sea against the English, but to carry soldiers to fight on English soil.

To be successful, Philip needed the Armada to call at the Netherlands to pick up a further 17,000 troops. It would then sail on to land somewhere in southern England, and the Spanish troops would march on London.

England prepares

Meanwhile, England was preparing itself for invasion. An army was stationed at the mouth of the River Thames in case the Spanish tried to reach London by river. Troops were also sent to guard the southern coast, and another force was sent to guard Queen Elizabeth I. Many beacons were built on hilltops along the south coast of England. They would be lit when the Armada was sighted, to give warning of the coming invasion.

Sir Francis Drake (1540–96). His method of sea warfare helped to revolutionize galleon design. The Spaniards called Drake El Draco or the Dragon.

Playing cat and mouse

England had several experienced seamen and military commanders. One of them was Sir Francis Drake, who had a plan to meet the Armada off the Cornish coast.

On July 29, 1588, Drake heard the news that the Armada had been sighted. With Lord Howard of Effingham (1536–1624), the English commander-in-chief, they sailed their fleet of 54 ships out of Plymouth. The two fleets sighted each other the following afternoon, but the signal for battle to begin did not come until the morning of July 31. Only a few shots were fired, and little damage was done. The English ships were lighter and faster than the huge Spanish galleons, which were like floating fortresses. So the English kept well out of range of the Spanish guns.

By accident, two Spanish galleons collided and were put out of action. One was captured by Drake and the captain and crew were taken prisoner. The second galleon had an explosion on board, and was towed away by the English.

The Armada sailed on up the Channel toward the Netherlands with the English fleet in pursuit, waiting for the right moment to attack. There were two more battles, but again little damage was done – the Spanish were frustrated that the English ships continued to keep out of range of their powerful guns.

After the third battle, the Spanish ships continued up the Channel and anchored off the French coast near Calais. There the English fleet saw their chance to make a decisive attack on the Armada.

Ordeal by fire

The English commanders had chosen to use the enemy sailors fear most – fire. With their sails unfurled and their rudders fixed in position, eight ships were set alight and released into the night so that the wind and tide would carry them into the Armada. Packed with explosives and shot, which exploded in all directions, they made a terrifying sight in the darkness.

Confusion and panic split the Spanish fleet apart. Ships were hastily cut free from their anchors and made

Queen Elizabeth I of England (1533–1603).

FASCINATING FACTS

The Armada carried six months' supply of food on board. It included 11 million pounds of ship's biscuits, 600,000 pounds of salt pork, 40,000 gallons of olive oil, and 14,000 barrels of wine.

❑

There is a story that when Sir Francis Drake heard that the Armada had been sighted off Cornwall, he was playing bowls on Plymouth Hoe. His reaction was to say, "Play out the game. There's time for that and to beat the Spanish after." There is no evidence that the story is true, but as it was low tide at Plymouth, Drake could not have sailed for several hours.

❑

Reporting on the failure of the Armada to Philip, the duke of Medina wrote: "The troubles and miseries we have suffered cannot be described to your Majesty. They have been greater than have ever been seen in any voyage before."

❑

Philip had been gathering the Armada together since the early 1850s. In 1580 he added Portugal to his Spanish empire and took over her navy, which included some of the finest fighting ships in the world.

❑

The duke of Medina-Sidonia's flagship was the San Martin de Portugal. She was a huge, 1,000-ton galleon carrying 48 guns.

for the open sea, some colliding with each other.

As dawn broke on August 8, the English could see that the neat formation of the Armada had been broken up and the ships lay strung out along several miles of the French coast. Drake could now lead the English attack in his ship, the *Revenge*.

Pounding the enemy
For nine hours that day, the English, with the wind behind them and hugely outnumbering the enemy, pounded at the helpless Armada. One huge Portuguese galleon, the *San Felipe*, was cut off and surrounded by English ships, which pulverized her with gunshot. Three Spanish galleons were sunk, and a dozen more badly holed.

When night fell, the English pulled

When the Armada moored off Calais, the English fleet immediately saw its advantage. With the help of a squadron of ships from Dover, Drake and Howard began to fill eight ships with explosives and material that would burn easily. With a favorable wind and tide, they planned to set the fireships so that they would drift into the ranks of the Spanish ships. It was after midnight when the Spaniards first saw the glowing fireships drifting toward them. The fireships caused great damage, but the confusion they wrought was just as important in the Armada's defeat.

away and prepared to renew the attack at dawn.

Exhausted, the Spanish sailors struggled against the wind and driving rain to keep their ships away from the sandbanks along the Flemish coast. But the next day the wind changed, allowing the Armada to escape northward up the North Sea. The English gave chase, and only turned back when they were satisfied that the Spanish were in retreat.

The Spanish admiral, Alonzo Duke of Medina-Sidonia, now faced a problem. His Armada was too weak to turn back and fight its way through the North Sea and the English Channel. In any case, the wind was blowing him northward. His only choice was to sail around Scotland into the Atlantic and then struggle home as best he could.

Battered by gale-force winds

The northwest coast of Scotland is famous for its stormy weather, and as it reached Cape Wrath, the Armada ran into gale-force winds. Twenty-five ships were driven onto the rocks.

Many of the wrecks were plundered by local people, and the surviving crew members killed. Some ships simply vanished without trace. Those ships that ploughed on through the Atlantic waves were crewed by fevered, starving sailors. The tattered remains of the Armada that finally returned to Spain had lost 64 ships and 11,000 men from the fleet that had so bravely set out three months before.

The end of an empire

The defeat of the Armada did not end Spain's power in Europe, but it was the beginning of the end. Over the next few years, Spain sent two more fleets to invade England, but both were defeated by storms.

The war between Catholic Spain and Protestant England dragged on, but Spain's attention was more and more taken up with holding on to its possessions rather than seeking new ones. The fireships of the English navy and the storms of the North Atlantic began the decline of Spain as a major European power.

In the first battle between the Spanish and English fleets, Lord Howard of Effingham attacked the leading flagship of the Armada in his own flagship, the Ark Royal.

Sobieski Saves Vienna

The weary defenders leaned on their spades and looked at the rough repair – they could do no more. Three months of siege had left the walls in ruins; the next Turkish attack would take Vienna. Looting and massacre would follow. Then, miraculously, on the mountain across the valley pinpoints of light appeared. Sobieski's army had arrived in the nick of time...

400	BC/AD	400	800	1200	1600	2000

1683 Vienna, Austria

Fear of the Ottoman Turks ran deep in eastern Europe. In a campaign in the 1520s, the Turks had overrun Hungary and had gone on to surround Austria's Vienna, only to be driven back by bad weather. Now, in 1683, they were on the march again.

Starving Vienna out

A huge Turkish army of 250,000 soldiers, led by Kara Mustafa, swept up the plain of the river Danube, looting, destroying, and slaughtering as they went.

In July, the Turks reached the walled city of Vienna and camped outside it. They settled down to starve the people of Vienna into surrender while pounding the walls away with their guns.

The Turks were so sure of an easy victory that Kara Mustafa and his officers arranged to live in silken tents decorated

John III Sobieski (1624–96) was a brilliant army commander. He was crowned king of Poland in 1674 and later led his cavalry against the Turks outside Vienna.

like palaces, with gardens in which they could stroll about. While they waited for Vienna to fall, their troops savagely burned and looted the surrounding countryside.

If Vienna had fallen, the Turks would have swept on up the Danube into the heart of Europe. Kara Mustafa boasted that he would not stop until his horses were stabled in St. Peter's Cathedral in Rome, the spiritual center of Christendom.

Hero of the hour

Two armies hurried to Austria to try to stop the Turkish advance. The Holy Roman Emperor's troops, under Duke Charles of Lorraine, marched from the west. They were often held up by the hordes of people fleeing east from Austria. But the hero of the hour was John Sobieski, king of Poland, who led his 26,000-strong, highly trained cavalry southward.

Meanwhile, Vienna was suffering terribly. Turkish guns pounded the city walls, while Turkish engineers tried to dig tunnels underneath them. The Austrian troops were outnumbered by about 10/1 by the Turks, but the ordinary citizens of the city were trained quickly to back up the full-time soldiers. Vienna's ordeal went on for three months until finally, on September 11, the walls crumbled and the city was about to fall.

In their tented camp that night, the Turks were jubilant – Vienna was theirs for the taking. But they rejoiced too soon. Suddenly the great wooded hill commanding the city was alight with the campfires of John Sobieski's army. The cavalry, led by the king himself, swooped down on the Turkish camp. Caught by surprise, the Turks panicked and fled, leaving behind all their weapons, ammunition, food, and loot. Even Kara Mustafa escaped with only one horse and in the clothes he was wearing. His own banner and battle honours, and all the treasure that he had looted, were left behind.

This was not the end of Sobieski and Leopold II's war against the Turks, but it was the turning point. Never again after 1683 were Vienna and Europe seriously threatened by an invasion from the Turks.

Although John Sobieski's arrival in the nick of time to save Christian Europe from the Turkish hordes made him a hero, the rest of his life was a disappointment. He could not trust either his nobles and courtiers at home or his allies abroad, and it is said that he died of a broken heart, having failed to make Poland strong enough to resist foreign invaders.

FASCINATING FACTS

A local merchant bought the coffee left by the Turks from the Polish army and used it to open the first of Vienna's famous coffeehouses.

After 1683 the Ottoman Turks were in retreat before Austria from the west and Russia from the north. Although the Ottoman Empire survived until 1918, it was never again a major threat to Europe.

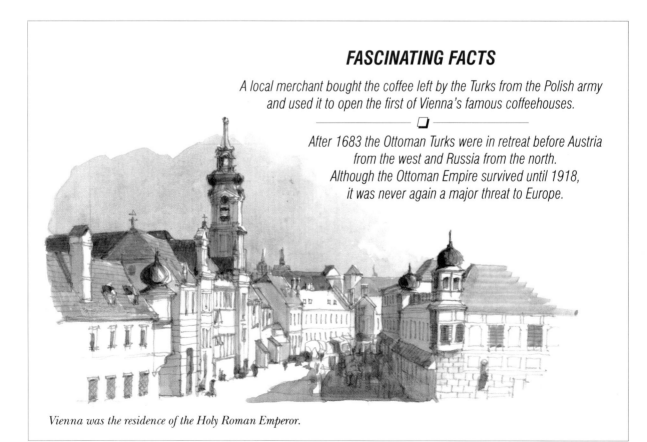

Vienna was the residence of the Holy Roman Emperor.

Wolfe Captures Quebec

A rumble, a thud, and a rattle of pebbles.... In the darkness soldiers froze, awaiting a sentry's challenge – but none came. Hearts pounding, they climbed on up the precipitous path. When dawn came, the little force was ready facing the French army outside Quebec. By sunset, French influence in Canada was ended, and Britain had a new colony.

400	BC/AD	400	800	1200	1600	2000

1759 Quebec, Montreal, Canada

The fight for Canada began when both the British and French wanted to open up the country for their own advantage and to gain from the fur trade, which was very profitable.

In 1663, the French had established a colony that they called New France, with Quebec as its capital. Britain had tried several times before, without success, to capture Quebec. In 1759 the British prime minister, William Pitt (1708–78), ordered General Wolfe to take command of a new attempt to take the settlement. Wolfe left England in February with a force of about 9,000 men.

Fight to the death

The British and French commanders were matched equally. At 32, Wolfe was remarkably young to have the rank of general, but he was very experienced in battle. His French opponent, General Louis de Montcalm (1712–59), was 15 years older and equally battle-hardened. For both, the battle of Quebec was to be literally a fight to the death.

Playing cat and mouse

The French troops were already dug in around Quebec when Wolfe and his men, sailing up the St. Lawrence River, arrived in the last week of June. There followed a frustrating two months of raids and counter-raids. The British troops, try as they might, could

James Wolfe (1727–59) was the son of a general. From the age of 14, he spent the whole of his life as a soldier, and himself rose to the rank of general.

Wolfe's plan to scale the cliffs called the Heights of Abraham near Quebec at night was a difficult and risky exercise, but it gave him the advantage of surprise that he needed in the battle against the French.

Both armies were helped by Native American allies.

neither dislodge the French from their defensive positions nor tempt them out to fight in the open.

By September, winter was about to set in. Wolfe was determined to settle the matter before the St. Lawrence froze over and movement in the harsh winter conditions became impossible. He made a daring plan. Under the cover of darkness, he would lead a force of 3,000 troops down the river to land at a little cove close by Quebec. Steep cliffs stood above the cove, and the French would not expect an attack from that direction.

Wolfe's plan worked marvelously. His men climbed the cliffs by a steep path, hauling their guns up behind them on ropes. When morning came, the British were massed for battle on the Plains of Abraham, in sight of the city of Quebec.

Surprise attack

The battle that followed was short. The British were outnumbered, but their muskets were superior to the French weapons, and they had the advantage of surprise.

British shot cut through the French ranks, and Montcalm's men quickly retreated, pursued by the British. Montcalm tried in vain to persuade his troops to turn and fight, but while he was doing so he was fatally wounded. He died not knowing that his enemy Wolfe, too, lay dead on the battlefield.

Five days later, the British occupied Quebec, and French rule in Canada was at an end. War with France was to continue for another 30 years, but the British victory at Quebec laid the foundation for the British Empire that was to control much of the world for the next century.

Washington After Lexington

"No taxation without representation!" was the watchword of the American colonists in 1775. They took up arms to defend their rights against the British oppressors and ended by founding a new nation. The general who masterminded their victory became the first president — his name was George Washington.

400	BC/AD	400	800	1200	1600	2000

1781 Yorktown, Virginia, USA

By the second half of the 18th century, the land that was to become the United States of America was under the control of Britain. It had been colonized by mostly British people who had chosen a better way of life away from their own country. But as the colonists grew wealthier and more sure of themselves, they became unhappy and wanted to be independent, or free of British rule.

The colonists' revolt

They resented the presence of a British army. They hated having to pay heavy taxes to the British and disliked British control of their trade. All these complaints led to a revolt in early 1775. But King George III (1738–1820) was determined to put down any rising and teach the rebels a lesson.

George Washington (1732–99) led the American army in the War of Independence against the British, and was twice elected president of the United States.

It would not be a fight against equal forces. The British had trained soldiers supported by a fleet. The colonists' army was made up of volunteers who were not as well trained or disciplined. But the colonists' forces included the "minutemen," so called because they were trained to be ready for action at a moment's notice.

Surprise attack?

The British had learned that the colonists in Massachusetts were raising and training a volunteer army. In April 1775, a force of British soldiers, known as "redcoats" because of the red tunics they wore, set out with orders to seize the colonists' armory at the settlement of Concord. The attack was intended to be a surprise, but was foiled by a Boston silversmith, Paul Revere. He rode through the night to warn the minutemen at Concord that the redcoats were coming.

A shot rings out

On April 18, when the British reached Lexington, a few miles from Concord, a shot rang out from behind a farm wall, and the redcoats fired back. The American War of Independence had begun.

Eight men, all colonists, were killed at Lexington, and the British marched on to Concord. By this time, the local minutemen were ready and waiting. In the fighting that followed, nearly 300 British soldiers were killed, almost three times as many as the losses of the colonists.

No going back

These were only the opening shots in the war. In June 1775 the first serious battle between the colonists and the British took place at Bunker Hill near Boston. Although they suffered terrible casualties, the British put the colonist army to flight. It was clear now that the British were determined to subdue the colonists at all costs. King George III himself had taken charge of Britain's war plans, and he had no sympathy with the Americans.

The colonists' leaders met urgently in Philadelphia to discuss the

In 1776, George Washington was chosen to lead America's revolutionary army. The infantry had no bayonets, the cavalry were ill-disciplined, and the only artillery were cannon won from the British army.

Washington is seen here accepting the British surrender at Yorktown in 1781. After this victory, it was only a matter of time before the Americans won the war.

FASCINATING FACTS

George Washington's family emigrated from England in 1657. The family home at Sulgrave, Northamptonshire, is now a museum.

▢

On July 4, Independence Day, the anniversary of the day on which the United States was founded, Americans celebrate with parades and fireworks.

▢

The tune played by the British military band as it led Cornwallis's troops back to camp after their surrender was called "The World Turned Upside Down." To the British, it must have seemed that that was just what the Americans had done by breaking away from British rule.

▢

George Washington was a rich man who had inherited large plantations and estates. When he became commander-in-chief of the army he refused pay. He did not earn a single dollar for his work during the war, although afterward the American Congress made him a generous grant of land.

▢

Among the rewards suggested for Washington after the war was that he should become king of the United States. He turned the idea down.

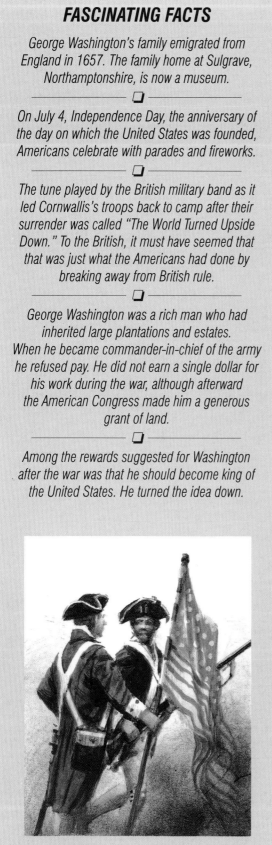

Minutemen of the American army.

situation. On July 4, 1776 they adopted the Declaration of Independence, which was a formal statement saying that America was an independent nation.

Washington leads the army
They also decided to raise an army and to put George Washington in charge of it. Washington, then 43, was an experienced soldier and a skilled administrator. He saw that his aim must be to forge a disciplined, highly trained army out of the 20,000 enthusiastic volunteers who had joined up. They were joined by volunteers from abroad, and later by troops and ships sent by the French government.

The war dragged on for several years with neither side gaining the upper hand. The British had their share of battle honors, but they suffered very heavy casualties. Early 1781 saw the British, under General Charles Cornwallis (1738–1805), firmly established at Yorktown, Virginia, near the mouth of Chesapeake Bay – the largest inlet in the Atlantic coast of North America. Washington and the French general Jean Rochambeau (1725–1807) marched to Yorktown, hoping to meet French troops that were arriving by sea.

Epic march
It was an epic march that Washington organized in his usual thorough way. Roads and bridges were repaired in advance, stores were set up, and river transport arranged.

Although the extra French troops failed to arrive, Washington pressed on, and, in early September, the 14,000-strong combined French and American army – twice the size of the

British force – was besieging Yorktown.

It must have been clear to an experienced general like Cornwallis that the British position was hopeless, but for several weeks he refused to give way. Washington ordered trenches to be dug close to the British lines, putting Cornwallis's troops in a stranglehold. In vain, the British attempted an evacuation by river, only to be foiled by bad weather.

King George III of England was determined to put down the colonists' revolt.

The British surrender

At last, on October 19, 1781, Washington received Cornwallis's formal surrender. At 2:00 P.M. the British troops marched out between the American and French lines to lay down their arms. Then they marched quietly back to camp, a defeated army. It was the high point of George Washington's military career.

The Boston Tea Party. In 1773, a group of colonists dressed as Native Americans boarded British ships and threw the cargo of tea into the harbor rather than pay duty on it.

The war was not yet over, but after the battle of Yorktown it was only a matter of time before the Americans won. Finally, in 1783, Britain signed the Treaty of Paris granting the United States of America their independence. This brought into being a nation that, in the 200 years since its creation, has become a major influence in world affairs.

First U.S. President

As for Washington, he would have liked to retire after the war to continue his life as a farmer. But the new nation needed his skills and wisdom, and in New York on April 30, 1789, he became the first president of the United States.

Napoleon Attacks Moscow

I have made a terrible mistake, thought Napoleon as he watched Moscow burn from the windows of the Kremlin. He ordered his superb army to retreat, but it was too late. Famine, disease, and winter weather took their toll on the soldiers, and hundreds of thousands died. The emperor of France, and overlord of most of Europe, had met his match at last.

400   BC/AD   400   800   1200   1600   2000

1812 Moscow, Russia

Napoleon's attack on Russia in 1812 was a gamble. Since becoming emperor of France in 1804, he had rarely lost a battle on land. He was a skillful and experienced battlefield commander, and he hoped and expected that the Russian army would meet him in battle as soon as his own troops crossed the Russian border.

If that had happened, Napoleon would almost certainly have won. His army, drawn from almost every corner of Europe, was 600,000 strong. It was better equipped and more highly trained than the forces of Alexander I (1777–1825), tsar of Russia, which numbered about 200,000.

The Russian trap
Things did not work out as Napoleon expected. Instead of challenging him, the Russians retreated, luring him

Napoleon Bonaparte (1769–1821) became a professional soldier when he was 16. A brilliant commander, he believed that he was invincible. But he was to die in exile.

deeper and deeper into Russian territory. The roads were bad, and supplies for the French army began to run out. Napoleon's soldiers had to march on empty stomachs. It was late summer – harvest time – but as the Russians retreated, they set their crops and farm buildings alight. Any hope of feeding the French army from Russian grain vanished. Starving, discontented soldiers deserted in their thousands.

Death at Borodino
Napoleon ordered his remaining soldiers to march on toward Moscow, the Russian capital. They reached Borodino, about 70 miles (115 kilometers) west of the city. There, the Russians stopped their retreat and turned to challenge their enemy. In the dreadful battle that followed, Napoleon lost 50,000 men and 30,000 horses, but after

Napoleon and his men had to retreat from Moscow through the terrible Russian winter. The invincible army was destroyed by hunger, snow, and cold.

FASCINATING FACTS

Napoleon had a habit of speaking through his nose, and his fellow cadets at the army training school nicknamed him "Straw-in-the-nose."

—————— ❏ ——————

A small, squat man with a pompous manner, Napoleon was given another nickname, "the little corporal," by his soldiers.

Early in his career, Napoleon was dismissed from the army by the French government. For a time he was so poor that he had to sell his books and watch.

—————— ❏ ——————

Napoleon's first wife was Josephine, whom he married in 1796. They had no children. In 1809 he divorced Josephine and married Marie Louise, an Austrian princess. They had one son. Josephine died in 1814. Marie Louise lived on until 1847.

10 hours of merciless fighting the Russians gave way. Such were Napoleon's powers of leadership that he was able to persuade his troops, despite their losses, hunger, and tiredness, to march on.

Moscow ablaze
In mid-September the French army arrived in Moscow, and Napoleon moved into the Kremlin, the center of government. But the people of Moscow were not going to submit to Napoleon and his unruly troops. Fires were started, destroying arms dumps – places where weapons are stored – and markets, and soon the whole of Moscow was alight. The city's people fled into the surrounding countryside, leaving Napoleon's soldiers stranded

in the city without food or weapons.
The harsh Russian winter was about to start. Too late, Napoleon saw that his attempt to add Russia to his empire had failed. In October he ordered a retreat. Over 100,000 soldiers started the long journey home, marching back past the burned countryside through which they had advanced.

The slow march home
It was terribly slow going. Napoleon's troops had to pass the battlefield of Borodino, where rotting bodies still lay in heaps and wounded men and horses still lay dying. The Russian winter was closing in, and before long snow began to fall. The Russian army launched attacks on the retreating French. To add to the misery, disease

broke out. Many died as the French army tried to ford ice-cold rivers.

Then a messenger brought Napoleon news of trouble back in Paris. There was a threat to his rule. He rode home as fast as possible, leaving his men to find their own way home. Many fell in the snow, starving and exhausted, and died where they lay. Extreme cold and hunger drove others mad. Many simply stumbled off into the snow and lost their way. The army that finally recrossed the Russian border numbered no more than about 25,000 men – only one in 25 of those who had set out.

End of a dream

It was one of the world's greatest military disasters, and the end of Napoleon's dream of conquering the world. He had been defeated by one of the most basic rules of warfare – keeping open good lines of supply – and by his own reckless ambition.

Gradually, his supporters at home and his allies abroad deserted him. Three years after the retreat from Moscow, Napoleon's empire had been broken up, and the man who hoped to rule the world was a prisoner on the island of St. Helena in the South Atlantic. He died in 1821, probably of cancer. But while his luck held, Napoleon had been one of history's greatest generals.

Napoleon and his men outside the Russian city of Moscow. At this moment it looked as if Napoleon was going to achieve his ambition to crush Russia, but within a month, his hungry, tired army was forced to begin an epic retreat, through a terrible winter, harassed by Russian soldiers. His forces were humiliated, and it was the end of his dream to rule the world.

Robert E. Lee & Sharpsburg

Civil war is the worst kind of war – it pits friend against friend, even brother against brother. At Sharpsburg, the Confederate and Union armies were led by old friends who fought ruthlessly against each other. That battle was a stalemate, but also a turning point. When Lee retreated south afterward, the fight to retain slavery in the United States was lost as well.

400	BC/AD	400	800	1200	1600	2000

1865 Sharpsberg, Maryland, USA

The United States of America was created by its leaders' Declaration of Independence in 1776. It was recognized by Britain and other nations in 1783. But within 60 years, it became clear that the Union of states was anything but united. There were deep divisions between the states in the North and those in the South.

Slavery or freedom?
The argument was partly about slavery. In the North there were no slaves. But the plantations in the South were worked by black slaves who lived and worked in terrible conditions – they had no rights and their owners had the power of life and death over them. As new states to the west were opened up, should slavery be allowed there or not?

Things came to a head in 1860 when Abraham

Lincoln (1809–65) was elected president of the United States. He had promised to abolish slavery in all states of the Union.

In 1861, in reply to this threat to their way of life, 11 southern states broke away from the Union. They formed their own government, the Confederacy, and elected Jefferson Davis (1808–89) as their own President.

The fight begins
On April 12, 1861 the Confederate army fired on the Union base at Fort Sumter in South Carolina – the Civil War had begun.

Whatever the rights and wrongs of their cause, the breakaway of the Southern states was an act of astonishing bravery. The North had the U.S. army on its side, and almost twice as many people from whom to draw new

General Robert E. Lee (1807–70) had been a soldier in the U.S. army since he was a young man, but resigned to become commander of the Confederate forces.

recruits. The army of the South was poorly equipped and badly clothed. Thousands of its troops had no shoes. But in the first battles of the war, the South scored many successes.

Crossing the Potomac

The Confederate president, Jefferson Davis, had as his military adviser General Robert E. Lee. Lee was a career soldier who had spent over thirty years in the U.S. army. He was quick to see that if the South had any chance of winning, its army must push north into Union territory instead of merely defending its own ground. But this meant crossing the Potomac River, which divided the Northern and Southern states.

It was a dangerous and difficult task. The Confederate army was short of men, food, weapons, ammunition, and horses. It would be fighting its way through hostile territory.

The Union in retreat

Late in August 1862, the two armies met at Bull Run, a small river in Virginia. A year earlier, Bull Run had seen a terrible battle in which nearly 5,000 soldiers had died. Then, the Confederate army had won, but had been too exhausted to follow up the victory with an advance northward. This time Lee was victorious again and sent the Union army in retreat to Washington. Lee was able to make the Potomac River crossing and press on into Maryland.

In its retreat, the Union army had left small garrisons (bodies of troops) behind to defend key places, including the river crossings. They were well dug in, and Lee decided that they would have to be removed before he

FASCINATING FACTS

Robert E. Lee almost fought on the Union side in the American Civil War. He believed in the Union, and President Lincoln was advised to offer him command of the Union forces. But Lee turned down the offer and, with great doubts about whether he was doing the right thing, became the commander of the Confederate army.

❏

Most soldiers come to hate their generals, but Lee was an exception. His troops would follow him anywhere, no matter how hungry or ill-equipped they were. One reason was that he was always ready to listen to them and share their miserable conditions.

❏

Four days after the battle at Antietam Creek, Abraham Lincoln proclaimed that from January 1, 1863, all slaves in the rebel states were to be recognized as free.

❏

The United States' main military cemetery, Arlington National Cemetery in Virginia, is on the south bank of the Potomac River. The land it occupies was once a plantation belonging to Lee's wife.

❏

General Ulysses S. Grant (1822–85), to whom Lee surrendered, later became the 18th president of the United States. He served from 1869 to 1877.

Ulysses S. Grant, General in Chief of the Union Army

continued his northward advance. At this point, he had a stroke of bad luck, or perhaps of betrayal.

The orders that went astray
Lee issued orders describing his plan on September 9, 1862. But some time over the next few days one copy of the orders went missing. It was discovered four days later by a Union soldier investigating an abandoned Confederate camp. He took it to an officer, who immediately sent it on to the Union general George B. McClellan (1826–85). And so Lee's plan fell into his enemy's hands.

The result was that a Union army of about 100,000 troops marched south to block Lee's advance at Antietam Creek, near Sharpsburg, Maryland. Lee had only 18,000 men, who were already exhausted from their struggle north. On September 17, the two armies faced each other, and the

Union opened the attack at dawn. With great skill and some good luck, Lee was able to hold out through the day until reinforcements arrived.

Although these made up an army only half the size of the Union's, Lee managed to avoid an outright defeat. But the day's battle had cost 26,000 lives – slightly more from the Union than from the Confederates – and Lee chose to stop the slaughter. He led his men back over the Potomac River,

On the afternoon of September 17, 1862, battle raged between Lee's Confederate troops and the Union army at Antietam Creek. Here the Union troops can be seen charging across the creek, forcing the Confederate army to retreat from the bank of the creek toward the town of Sharpsburg. Lee then decided to stop the slaughter and led his men away from the battlefield. Like many battles in the war, thousands of soldiers had died, but no one side could claim a real victory. The United States was bleeding to death in a murderous civil war.

leaving Maryland to the Union.

The battle of Antietam Creek was like so many battles in the American Civil War. Neither side could claim a real victory, but thousands of lives had been lost. The war still had almost three years to run, and there would be thousands more deaths as well as untold misery for the wounded.

Fighting old friends

Lee was not one of those generals who care nothing for the suffering of their soldiers. He knew that his men were sick of fighting on empty stomachs, with poor equipment, and without knowing when their next supplies would arrive. The Union had successfully stopped foreign supply ships from reaching Confederate ports.

He knew too that many of his troops, like himself, were fighting against soldiers who had once been their friends. Earlier in his career, he had fought alongside General Ulysses S. Grant, the great Union general.

Meanwhile, the cost of the war mounted. Both sides were forced to order men into the army instead of relying on volunteers. The land over which battles were fought became useless for farming. No one knows for certain how many soldiers died, but some historians have estimated that it was over 1 million. Of these, two died of disease caused by conditions on the battlefield for every one who died in battle.

President Abraham Lincoln was shot by J. Wilkes Booth a week after Lee's surrender.

Surrender!

The end came in April 1865. Steady advances by Union forces had worn the Confederate army down to about 30,000 men. Lee and his troops arrived at the village of Appomattox in Virginia, expecting to find supplies waiting for them. None had arrived. It was too early in the year to find food in the fields. The Confederate soldiers were starving and in no condition to face yet another hard-fought battle.

There was only one answer. Lee ordered one of his officers to ride forward to offer surrender. No white flag could be found, so a towel was used instead. Lee and Grant, old friends who had become enemies, sat down together to work out the terms of surrender. Confederate troops were not to be punished. They could return home to make a living as best they could. Lee himself spent the last five years of his life teaching in college.

Building a nation

Americans from North and South set about the task of putting their nation together again. But the act of a madman made the task more difficult. A week after Lee's surrender, President Lincoln celebrated the end of the war by going to the theater. As he sat watching the play he was shot, and died the next morning. The war had been won by the Union, but the struggle to make America a nation of united states had only just begun.

Kruger's Boers Against Britain

"Mafeking is relieved," shouted the jubilant crowds in London in May 1900.
Bonfires were lit and people danced in the streets, but the war
far away in South Africa was not over. The Boers fought on stubbornly and won
concessions from the British that allowed the later development of apartheid.
Paul Kruger's legacy still influences South Africa today....

400	BC/AD	400	800	1200	1600	2000

1901 Mafeking, South Africa

The dispute between the Boers – the descendants of Dutch and other colonists in southern Africa – and the British dated back to 1815. As part of the peace settlement following the Napoleonic Wars, the Dutch colony at the Cape of Good Hope was handed over to Britain. Soon, new British settlers arrived, and to escape British rule many Boers moved northward to found new territories of their own.

In 1881 the Boer state of the Transvaal gained independence from Britain. Two years later, Paul Kruger, former chief of the Transvaal army, became president of the independent state.

Flashpoint

By 1899, after years of disputes, the situation between the Boers and the British had reached a point when violence was inevitable. Britain was openly interfering in Transvaal's affairs and was preparing troops to be shipped out to South Africa to reinforce the small army that was already there. But before the reinforcements could arrive, the Boers seized their chance. With an army of 35,000 men, they crossed into British territory.

British plans dashed

The attack was a disaster for the British because its army was smaller than the Boers' army. Nearly one-third of the British troops – 10,000 men – were trapped in their headquarters at the border town of Ladysmith.

The quick victory that the British had hoped for and expected was now out of the question. The Boers were well armed, with German heavy guns, and they had the

Paul Kruger (1825–1904) led the Boers' fight for independence from Britain. From 1883 he was president of the Boer territory of the Transvaal.

advantage of knowing the country over which they were fighting. Soon, the Boers had surrounded two other key towns, Mafeking and Kimberley.

Desperate measures

Britain now began to pour all its effort into the war. Reinforcements arrived in southern Africa from other parts of the British Empire, but the Boers held on to their gains.

Britain was desperate to end the war quickly. More volunteers were called for at home, but many had to be rejected for army service because they were unfit. In December 1899, the British commander, General Sir Redvers Buller, was replaced by Field Marshal Lord Roberts (1832–1914), with Lord Kitchener (1850–1916) as his chief of staff.

The tide turns

From then on, the war turned against the Boers, although they still scored some successes. Lord Roberts concentrated his forces instead of spreading them thinly as Buller had done. Kimberley was relieved (the siege was lifted) on February 15, 1900, and on February 28, Ladysmith was also relieved.

Help had come in the nick of time for the people of Ladysmith. Disease had broken out and the town could

British soldiers defending the town of Ladysmith on the Natal border against Boer troops. The Boers knew the country and used this to their advantage, sticking to their task with determination. Almost one-third of the 10,000 British troops died in the siege, which lasted for four months in 1899–1900. The Boers were eventually driven back by advancing British forces led by Field Marshall Lord Roberts.

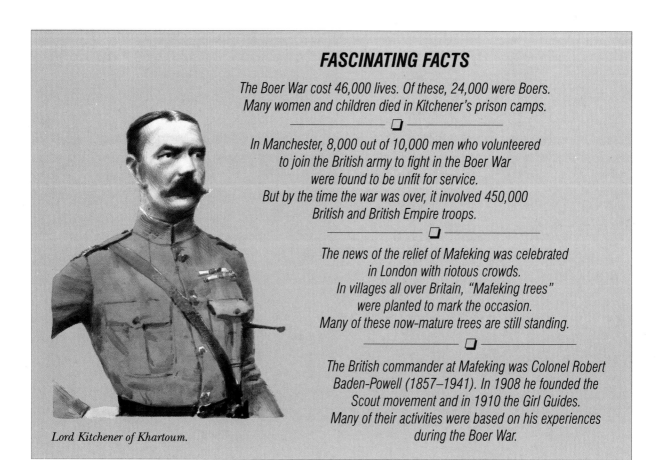

FASCINATING FACTS

The Boer War cost 46,000 lives. Of these, 24,000 were Boers. Many women and children died in Kitchener's prison camps.

In Manchester, 8,000 out of 10,000 men who volunteered to join the British army to fight in the Boer War were found to be unfit for service. But by the time the war was over, it involved 450,000 British and British Empire troops.

The news of the relief of Mafeking was celebrated in London with riotous crowds. In villages all over Britain, "Mafeking trees" were planted to mark the occasion. Many of these now-mature trees are still standing.

The British commander at Mafeking was Colonel Robert Baden-Powell (1857–1941). In 1908 he founded the Scout movement and in 1910 the Girl Guides. Many of their activities were based on his experiences during the Boer War.

Lord Kitchener of Khartoum.

not have held out for much longer.

The British advance swept on. Mafeking was relieved on May 17 – it had been under siege for 217 days. By August 1900, the Boer army was defeated and Paul Kruger fled to Europe.

But this was not the end of Boer resistance. Small bands continued the fight, attacking supply convoys, railways, and British camps for another year and a half. They were only defeated when Lord Kitchener, who was now in charge, set up a network of guard houses covering the whole country. Large numbers of Boers who were suspected of helping the bands

Boer guerrillas knew the country well.

were rounded up and held in prison camps. One in five of these prisoners died, mostly of disease.

Uneasy peace

A peace treaty was finally signed on May 31, 1902. It gave the Boers personal freedom under British rule, and there was no punishment for those who had taken part in the war.

But it was an agreement only between the Boers and the British. The settlement ignored the question of the rights of the native black peoples of southern Africa. The whites continued to exploit them and treat them as second-class citizens.

The Start of World War I

"Austria mobilizing," read the telegrams from Berlin, "Germany backs her. Advise our plans advanced." As the armies began to roll across Europe, the most terrible war of all time was underway. Sparked by two assassinations in Sarajevo, Bosnia, the world was about to be plunged into four years of bloodshed.

| 400 | BC/AD | 400 | 800 | 1200 | 1600 | 2000 |

1914 Sarajevo, Bosnia

The war that began in 1914 had been threatened for many years – rivalry between the great European powers lay behind it. In the 1870s, Germany and Italy had become unified nations instead of groups of separate states. They had new energy and ambitions.

There had been a bitter border dispute between Germany and France, which led to war in 1870. Russia, which was slow to industrialize, was becoming more prosperous. Britain and Germany were rivals in the colonization of Africa.

Alliances across Europe

The European powers had made alliances that were supposed to keep the peace. In fact, each alliance was aimed at controlling the other powers. France, Britain, and Russia were allied against Germany, Austria-Hungary, and Italy. These agreements meant that each country in an alliance would help the others if they were threatened.

Fight for the cause

Meanwhile, there was trouble in southeastern Europe. The Austro-Hungarian Empire was made up of many different ethnic groups, such as the Czechs, Poles, Jews, and Serbs. They wanted power and independence. The Serbs in particular formed secret groups to fight for their cause in both Serbia and neighboring Bosnia. Both states were occupied by Austro-Hungarian troops, but it began to look as if only an all-out invasion of Serbia would crush the underground movement.

Kaiser Wilhelm II (1859–1941) became emperor of Germany in 1888. He abdicated at the end of World War I and retired to the Netherlands until his death.

Fateful visit

Early in 1914, the Austro-Hungarians decided to send the emperor's nephew, Archduke

Francis Ferdinand, to Bosnia. The plan was that he would inspect the imperial troops and try to make peace with the Serbs. One of the highlights of the visit was to be a ceremonial drive through the Bosnian capital, Sarajevo.

The day chosen for the ceremonial drive was June 28. As it happened, it was the wedding anniversary of the archduke and his wife Sophie. On the ride through Sarajevo, a bomb was thrown at their open car, but it missed them. The archduke and his wife were advised to stay under cover for the rest of the day, but they went out again.

The wrong turning

On the archduke's second journey, his driver took a wrong turning. He stopped the car and reversed. This brought the archduke and Sophie face to face with a 19-year-old Serbian student, Gavrilo Princip (1895–1918), who was standing in the street.

Princip was not just an ordinary passerby. Although his presence in the street at that moment must have been accidental, he was a member of a protest group and had been given a pistol by the Serbian underground

Gavrilo Princip (right) being led away after he had jumped on to the running board of the open car and shot dead Archduke Francis Ferdinand and his wife Sophie. The Serb underground movement in Bosnia had supplied the pistol to Princip, who died in an Austrian prison. The assassination caused the Austro-Hungarian Empire to declare war on Serbia on July 28, 1914. By August 4 Britain had declared war on Germany and all the major European nations were at war.

Much of World War I's fighting was carried out in the trenches of the Western Front. These stretched from the Belgian coast to the Swiss frontier. Millions died in those trenches to gain perhaps a few yards of ground.

Sir John Haig of Britain and Marshal Foch of France watch over the killing fields of no-man's-land.

FASCINATING FACTS

The kings of the two major enemies, Kaiser Wilhelm II of Germany and King George V of Britain, were cousins, and before the war had been friends.

❏

Fighting in World War I happened in Europe, the Middle East, parts of Africa, and even the Far East. By 1917, the Western Front, 450 miles (725 kilometers) long, wound its way from the Swiss border to the North Sea.

❏

The first use of poison gas was by German troops against the French army on April 22, 1915.

❏

On July 1, 1916, the British army attacked the German positions along the River Somme in northern France. The casualties on the battle's first day were horrific – over 57,470 men were either killed or wounded.

❏

Tanks were first used by the British army during the Battle of the Somme on September 15, 1916.

❏

American troops arrived on June 25, 1917, and fought along with British and French troops until the Armistice (final ceasefire) at 11:00 A.M. on November 11, 1918.

movement. As he leapt on to the car's running board he raised the pistol and fired two shots at the archduke and his wife. They died almost at once.

War is declared

As a fire can spread from a single spark, so World War I spread unavoidably from those two shots in Sarajevo. With German backing, Austria declared war on Serbia. Russia mobilized her troops. Germany declared war on Russia and began to threaten France. The promises that Britain made to help France and Russia if they were threatened now had to be honored, and on August 4, 1914, Britain declared war on Germany. Every major power in Europe was now involved.

The price of war

Everyone expected a short, sharp war. People told each other that it would all be over by Christmas. They were wrong. World War I dragged on for four terrible years. No one knows exactly how many lives were lost in the war, but it was probably about 10 million people. Added to this were the millions who were blinded, gassed, or crippled, and who would never live normal lives again.

Yet, because it was so terrible, the war did bring about a desire all over the world to settle disputes between nations by peaceful means. The first attempt to set up an organization to bring this about, the League of Nations, failed. But before 1914, generals and statesmen of all nationalities never questioned that war was the way to settle disputes between nations. After 1918, many realized that it should be the last resort.

Japan Bombs Pearl Harbor

"Tora, tora, tora," cried the Japanese squadron leader as he led the first wave of bombers diving to attack Pearl Harbor. Two hours later the Americans had lost 18 ships, 177 aircraft, and thousands of dead and wounded. The "European" war that Americans had tried to avoid had reached out and struck home to them. It was a world war at last.

400	BC/AD	400	800	1200	1600	2000

1941 Pearl Harbor, Hawaii

Pearl Harbor was the headquarters of the U.S. Pacific Fleet. At around 7:00 A.M. on the morning of December 7, 1941, a radar operator at the base, keeping a routine watch, noticed blips of approaching aircraft on his screen. He thought they must be American planes on a training exercise and did not alert anyone of the approaching aircraft.

About half an hour later, a sailor on watch on one of the ships in the harbor saw some aircraft approaching, but he too thought nothing of it. At 7:55 A.M. a Japanese dive-bomber shrieked down on the defenseless base and the first bombs fell.

Waves of terror

Most of the U.S. Pacific Fleet was at anchor in the harbor. The crews were on shore leave and the guns were unmanned. The alarm was raised just as the first bombs tore

Hideki Tojo (1884–1948) was Japan's prime minister and commander-in-chief in 1941. After the end of the war, he was tried and executed as a war criminal.

into the American warships. Wave after wave of Japanese aircraft followed, raining bombs down onto the helpless fleet. Meanwhile, several Japanese submarines had also arrived and fired torpedoes at the U.S. ships.

Aftermath of the attack

By 10:00 A.M. the raid was over. In all, 18 warships were sunk or badly damaged. The bombers also attacked the base airfield, Hickam Field, and destroyed many of the aircraft that were standing idle on the ground. Nearly 2,500 servicemen were killed. Almost 1,000 more were reported missing, and over 1,200 were wounded.

There was only one piece of good news. It happened that the U.S. Navy's two aircraft carriers were at sea, and so survived the attack.

The first wave of Japanese airplanes bombarded the U.S. Pacific Fleet for about 30 minutes. Fortunately for the Americans, their two aircraft carriers were at sea, and so were not damaged in the attack.

The United States strikes back

The surprise attack had been ordered by General Tojo, Japan's prime minister and commander-in-chief of the Japanese forces. The United States had become increasingly alarmed about Japanese conquests in southeast Asia. Here was a chance to inflict serious damage on U.S. forces before they were ordered to attack Japan. General Tojo knew that bombing Pearl Harbor would provoke the United States to go to war, but he believed that Japan was strong enough to win.

When President Roosevelt declared war on Japan after the attack, General Tojo appealed to Germany for help. Soon Germany and the United States were also at war. A long struggle to defeat Japan, Germany, and their other ally, Italy, had begun.

The long struggle

It was almost four years before Germany, and finally Japan, were defeated by the Allies. The Japanese, with their belief in fighting to the death, were the most stubborn enemy. They surrendered only when, in August 1945, the U.S. Air Force dropped two atomic bombs on Japan and threatened to drop more. But it was the Japanese strike at Pearl Harbor that brought the United States into World War II, and so helped to create the world we know today.

FASCINATING FACTS

Peace talks between Japan and the United States were broken off only hours before the Pearl Harbor attack. But the leaders of both countries knew that war was unavoidable. What the Americans did not know was that Japanese aircraft carriers were already in position.

———— ❏ ————

The Japanese attack was launched from six aircraft carriers stationed 250 miles (400 kilometers) north of Pearl Harbor.

———— ❏ ————

Eighty-six ships were anchored in Pearl Harbor on December 7, 1941. Five battleships and five other warships were sunk. Three more battleships, three cruisers, and two other ships were badly damaged.

On the airfield, 177 aircraft were lost. Japanese losses were 48 aircraft and 3 submarines.

———— ❏ ————

During the attack on Pearl Harbor, the battleship Arizona *was sunk, the* West Virginia *was badly holed, and the* Oklahoma *capsized. The* California *sank into the mud so that only her superstructure (the part of a ship above the main deck) could be seen.*

———— ❏ ————

Pearl Harbor was so unprepared for attack that fire-fighting equipment and ammunition for the base guns were locked away. Servicemen tried to down the Japanese aircraft with rifle fire.

Eisenhower & D-Day

Cold, nervous, and seasick, the Allied soldiers aboard the hundreds of landing craft waited for dawn. Waves of aircraft rumbled overhead, and as the sun rose, fighter planes screamed in to attack the German defenses. Then the landing craft hit the beaches – soldiers and tanks charged ashore. The Allies' offensive against the Third Reich had finally started.

400	BC/AD	400	800	1200	1600	2000

1944 Normandy, France

In April and May 1944, a huge force of over 3.5 million American, Canadian, and British troops began to assemble along the coast of southern England. Gathered in makeshift camps, with their tanks and equipment hidden under trees, they were waiting for the signal to move.

At the same time, 13,000 aircraft were assembled on southern airfields, and a vast invasion fleet gathered in southern ports. All leave was canceled. Those who were not in the armed forces were kept out of the way as much as possible, and travel to the south coast was banned.

Defeat the Axis

Preparations were under way for the invasion of France by the combined Allied forces. Since 1940, France and most of western Europe had been occupied – taken and held – by Germany. It was time now to land, drive the Germans back, defeat them on their own territory, and so end World War II in Europe.

The invasion is planned

Planning for the invasion had been going on for two years in the greatest detail. No one imagined that the invasion – the largest naval invasion in history – would be easy. Only two armies, those of the Romans and the Normans, had ever achieved an invasion across the English Channel, and they were facing a weak and divided England. The Allies would be attacking well-defended beaches through minefields and heavy enemy fire.

The Allies would have only one chance. If they failed, the Germans would drive them back

General Dwight D. Eisenhower (1890–1969) had been in the U.S. Army all his working life. After World War II, he became the 34th president of the United States (1953–61).

into the sea, where they would be trapped. The future history of Europe depended on the Allies' success.

A U.S. Army general, Dwight D. Eisenhower, was in charge of the whole invasion plan, which was codenamed "Operation Overlord." A British general, Bernard Montgomery (1887–1976), was picked to command the land forces.

Daring ideas

Many new and daring ideas played a part in the plan. One was a flexible pipe that was laid on the seabed of the English Channel to carry fuel supplies to the forces once they had landed. Another was the building of two floating harbors that were towed to France to make the landing of the huge army easier. Tanks were specially adapted to clear mines, attack concrete defenses, and lay bridges.

False trails

All these preparations, and the assembly of the invasion forces, had to be carried out in total secrecy. At the same time, false information was leaked to Germany about Allied plans.

This led the Germans to believe that the invasion would take place in the Pas de Calais on the northeast coast of France. In fact, it was planned for Normandy, to the west. The U.S. Army would attack beaches that were codenamed Utah and Omaha, the Canadians would land on Juno, and the British on Gold and Sword.

By June, all was ready, and Eisenhower named June 5 as D-Day, the day of the invasion. But on the day before, gales lashed the sea, and the beaches were shrouded in fog.

To have attempted an invasion

Paratroops landed at key points behind enemy lines.

FASCINATING FACTS

The force gathered on the south coast of England included 4,000 assault craft, 1,200 warships, and 1,600 merchant ships.

❏

Days before the invasion, the Times newspaper of London printed a crossword in which several of the code words to be used on D-Day appeared as answers. There was alarm at Eisenhower's headquarters. Was someone using the Times to pass secret information?
On investigation, it turned out that the person who had made up the crossword had chosen the words completely by accident.

❏

The Allies built fleets of dummy ships made of wood, which were moored in harbors on the southeast coast of England to convince the Germans that the invasion would take place on the coast of the Pas de Calais.
On D-Day itself, Allied bombers carried out raids there to keep up the deception.

❏

The number of Allied troops who landed in Normandy before nightfall on D-Day was 155,000. Twice as many were in France by the end of the first week.

under those conditions would have been disastrous. But weather forecasters predicted a "weather window" – a short period of fine weather – for June 6. On the evening before, Eisenhower gave the order for the invasion to begin.

Troops embarked on 4,000 landing craft. A fleet of 1,200 warships moved into position to cover the invaders, and 1,600 merchant ships were ready to follow up the invasion with supplies. As the ships slipped away from England in the gathering night, troops boarded gliders that would carry them to key points inland.

Dawn shock

German soldiers guarding the Normandy coast spent an uneasy night. Wave after wave of Allied aircraft throbbed overhead. Soon, there was news that paratroops and gliders had landed inside France. When the sun rose, it revealed what the Germans had feared most. Out at sea, stretching away to the horizon, was a vast fleet of ships.

Almost at once, the assault began. Rockets and shells from the Allied warships tore at the German defenses. The sky filled with bombers, which targeted the concrete gun positions and machine-gun posts along the coast. Following up these attacks, the first landing craft reached the beaches and began to unload men, tanks and heavy guns.

British troops help their wounded comrades ashore at Sword Beach in Normandy. The D-Day landings were a crucial point in the war, during which the Allies seized the initiative, and after which German success was limited. It was the beginning of the end of the war.

Meanwhile, the airborne troops had landed and captured important bridges and other key installations inland. A temporary airfield was quickly set up to receive more gliders carrying heavy equipment.

Trouble at Omaha

But not everything went according to plan. The American troops who attacked the Omaha beach at St. Laurent ran into difficulties with heavy seas. The waves disrupted the landing, and many lives were lost as the men crawled ashore wet, cold, and under heavy enemy fire. But the Utah force, and the three British forces, landed quickly and successfully. By nightfall, they had overcome the German defenses and pushed on several miles inland.

Meanwhile, the secret invasion was a secret no longer. All over the world, people woke up to hear on their radios the news that D-Day had arrived. In Europe, where millions of people lived under German occupation, a great sigh of relief went up. People greeted each other excitedly, "They have landed!" The defeat of Germany and its hated leader, Adolf Hitler, was in sight.

Drive on Berlin

The D-Day invasion was only the beginning of a long campaign to drive the Germans out of France and the other occupied countries of western Europe. There were some setbacks in store for the Allies as the Germans threw all their forces into defending Germany itself. But by early 1945, the final assault on Germany had begun.

In April, the Allied forces met the Russian army, which had advanced on Germany from the east. On May 1, realizing that defeat was only days away, Adolf Hitler killed himself. Six days later the Germans surrendered, and next day there was dancing in the streets all over Europe.

Thanks to careful planning and the superb leadership of Eisenhower and Montgomery, the D-Day invasion that had begun with outline plans made over two years before had reached a triumphant conclusion.

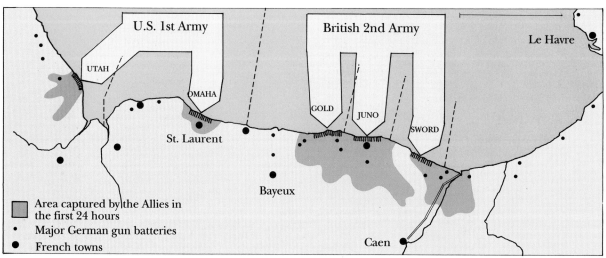

The D-Day invasion beaches, June 6, 1944. The invasion army was split into five forces: the American forces were codenamed Utah and Omaha, and the three British forces were codenamed Gold, Juno, and Sword.

Further Reading

Anderson, David. *The Spanish Armada.* New York: Hampsted Press, 1988

Bruns, Roger. *George Washington.* New York: Chelsea House, 1987.

Chu, Daniel, and Elliot Skinner. *A Glorious Age in Africa.* Trenton, NJ: Africa World Press, 1990.

Clark, Philip. *American Civil War.* Palo Alto, CA: Cherrytree, 1988.

Dank, Milton. *D-Day.* New York: Franklin Watts, 1984.

Devaney, John. *America Goes to War 1941.* New York: Walker, 1991.

Ellacott, S. E. *The Norman Invasion.* New York: Abelard-Schuman, 1966.

Hill, Ken. *World War I.* Palo Alto, CA: Cherrytree, 1988.

Hull, Robert, ed. *A Prose Anthology of the First World War.* Brookcreek, CT: Millbrook Press, 1993.

Humphrey, Judy. *Gengis Khan.* New York: Chelsea House, 1987.

Jackson, John G. *Introduction to African Civilizations.* New York: Citadel Press/Carol, 1970.

Jessop, Joanne. *Crusaders.* Denver, CO: Wayland, 1989.

Langley, Andrew. *Genghis Khan and the Mongols.* Denver, CO: Wayland, 1988.

McGuire, Leslie. *Napoleon.* New York: Chelsea House, 1986.

Marrin, Albert. *The War for Independence: The Story of the American Revolution.* New York: Atheneum, 1988.

Martin, Colin. *Full Fathom Five: Wrecks of the Spanish Armada.* New York: Viking, 1975.

Millard, Anne. *The Usborne Book of World History.* Tulsa, OK: Usborne, 1985.

Pacoe, Elaine. *South Africa: Troubled Land.* New York: Franklin Watts, 1987.

Peach, Susan, and Anne Millard. *The Greeks.* Tulsa, OK: Usborne, 1990.

Riley-Smith, Jonathan. *The Crusades: A Short History.* New Haven, CT: Yale University Press, 1987.

Sandberg, Peter Lars. *Dwight D. Eisenhower.* Chelsea House, 1986.

Severns, Karen. *Hirohito.* New York: Chelsea House, 1988.

Simpson, Jacqueline. *Everyday Life in the Viking Age.* New York: Dorset Press, 1967.

Smith, Alice E. *Sir Francis Drake and the Struggle for an Ocean Empire.* New York: Chelsea House, 1993.

Speed, Peter. *Harald Hardrada and the Vikings.* Palo Alto, CA: Cherrytree, 1992.

Stefoff, Rebecca. *The Viking Explorers.* New York: Chelsea House, 1993.

Sullivan, George. *The Day Pearl Harbor Was Bombed: A Photo History of World War II.* New York: Scholastic, 1991.

Traub, James. *India: The Challenge of Change.* New York: Messner, 1981.

Várdy, Steven Béla. *Attila.* New York: Chelsea House, 1991.

Wavel, Geoffry C., et al. *The Civil War: An Illustrated History.* New York: Borzoi/Knopf, 1990.

Index